DECADES OF THE
20TH
CENTURY

1960s

ELDORADO INK

DECADES OF THE 20TH CENTURY

1900s

1910s

1920s

1930s

1940s

1950s

1960s

1970s

1980s

1990s

DECADES OF THE
20TH CENTURY

1960s

ELDORADO INK

Published by Eldorado Ink
2099 Lost Oak Trail
Prescott, AZ 86303
www.eldoradoink.com

Milan Bobek, Editor
Judith C. Callomon, Historical consultant
Samuel J. Patti, Consulting editor

Printed and bound in Slovenia

Publisher Cataloging Data

1960s / [Milan Bobek, editor].
       p. cm. -- (Decades of the 20th century)
     Includes index.
     Summary: This volume, arranged chronologically, presents
key events that have shaped the decade, from significant political
occurrences to details of daily life.
     ISBN 1-932904-06-9
     1. Nineteen sixties   2. History, Modern--20th century--
Chronology   3. History, Modern--20th century--Pictorial works
I. Bobek, Milan   II. Title: Nineteen sixties   III. Series
     909.82/6--dc22

Picture research and photography by Anne Hobart Lang and Rolf
Lang of AHL Archives. Additional research by Heritage Picture
Collection, London.

CONTENTS

THE SWINGING SIXTIES

The 1960s witness a creative explosion of popular culture and a major shift in attitudes to personal and public morality. In the United States, there is a new Camelot with President Kennedy in the royal role. For a decade in pursuit of peace, love, and understanding, there is a remarkable amount of violence: revolutions, riots, protests, assassinations, and demonstrations abound. In America and Africa, black people assert their rights. Energy and optimism are directed upwards as the Soviet Union and the United States race each other to conquer space.

OPPOSITE: Civil rights protests and demonstrations characterize the decade.

1960–1969

KEY EVENTS OF THE DECADE

- SHARPEVILLE MASSACRE
- JOHN F. KENNEDY ASSASSINATED
- CONTRACEPTIVE PILL
- HUMANITY IN SPACE
- THE CUBAN CRISIS
- THE BERLIN WALL
- BLACK CIVIL RIGHTS
- VIETNAM WAR
- THE BEATLES
- MINISKIRTS

- BLACK POWER
- UDI IN RHODESIA
- POLIO VACCINE
- PRAGUE SPRING
- SUMMER OF LOVE
- THE SIX DAY WAR
- STUDENT PROTEST
- MEN ON THE MOON

WORLD POPULATION 3,109 MILLION

WINDS OF CHANGE START TO BLOW

The decade starts as it means to go on, as liberation of all kinds scents the breeze. In Africa, European colonial power evaporates as more countries gain independence. Only South Africa bucks the trend, with white minority rule cracking down on the black populace. In the United States, a dynamic young president is elected. Italian director Federico Fellini anticipates the sexual revolution with his film *La Dolce Vita*, while in Britain, D.H. Lawrence's *Lady Chatterley's Lover* is declared a good (and legal) read.

1960

Jan	**4**	French author Albert Camus dies in a car crash at age 46
	8	Kenneth Kaunda is freed from jail in Northern Rhodesia (Zambia); he later becomes president
	23	Bathyscaphe *Trieste* makes record dive of some 30,000 feet in Marianas Trench
Feb	**18**	Eighth Winter Olympics open at Squaw Valley, California
Mar	**30**	Sharpeville Massacre: South African police panic and kill 56 black protesters
Apr	**1**	First weather satellite, *Tiros 1*, is launched
May	**1**	Soviets shoot down U.S. U-2 spy plane over the Ural Mountains
	30	Russian author Boris Pasternak dies
June	**30**	Belgian Congo becomes independent as Congo Republic
Aug	**16**	British colony of Cyprus becomes an independent republic
Nov	**8**	John F. Kennedy is elected 35th U.S. President

ABOVE: Democratic Senator John F. Kennedy is President-elect.

АППАРАТУРА РАДИОРАЗВЕДКИ
ДЛЯ РАЗВЕДКИ НАЗЕМНЫХ РАДИОЛОКАЦИОННЫХ
СТАНЦИЙ
ДИАПАЗОНЫ ВОЛН:
САНТИМЕТРОВЫЙ, ДЕЦИМЕТРОВЫЙ И МЕТРОВЫЙ
УЗЛЫ ИЗГОТОВЛЕНЫ:
ЛАБОРАТОРИЕЙ ХАГГИНС (МЕНЛОУ-ПАРК, КАЛИФОРНИЯ)
ХЬЮЛЕТТ-ПАККАРД К° (ПАЛО АЛЬТО, КАЛИФОРНИЯ)
МИКРОЛАБ, РЕЙТЕОН, СИЛЬВАНИЯ

AIRBORNE RADIO-RECONNAISSANCE EQUIPMENT
DESIGNED FOR RECONNAISSANCE
OF THE   GROUND RADARS
WAVE BANDS: MICRO, DECIMETRIC AND METER
MFG: HUGGINS LABS, MENLO PARK, CALIFORNIA,
HEWLETT-PACKARD Co, PALO ALTO
CALIFORNIA, MICROLAB, RAYT

АНТЕННА MP 11719
АППАРАТУРЫ РАДИОРАЗВЕДКИ
НАЗЕМНЫХ РАДИОЛОКАЦИОННЫХ СТАНЦИЙ
10-см ДИАПАЗОНА РАДИОВОЛН

MP 11719 АНТЕННА

ABOVE: Wreckage from the alleged U.S. U-2 spy plane shot down in Russian airspace goes on display in Moscow.

AN END TO WHITE RULE IN AFRICA

Cameroon gains its independence from France. Over the next 11 months, 13 former French colonies, Somalia (combining former British and Italian colonies), and Nigeria all gain their independence. In June, the Belgian colony of the Congo becomes independent as the Congo Republic with Patrice Lumumba as prime minister. Visiting South Africa, British prime minister Harold Macmillan states that a "wind of change" is blowing through the continent, with black African states gaining independence and white rule ending.

MASSACRE IN THE TOWNSHIP

Police open fire against demonstrators in the black township of Sharpeville, south of Johannesburg, killing 56 Africans and injuring 162. The demonstrators were protesting against the newly passed laws requiring all Africans to carry an identity pass at all times. As a result of the massacre, the African National Congress (ANC) and the Pan-African Congress (PAC) are banned. International protests force South Africa to leave the British Commonwealth and become an independent republic in May 1961, increasing the international isolation of the apartheid government.

EICHMANN FOUND

Israeli intelligence officers kidnap Adolf Eichmann, the SS officer who masterminded the Final Solution in Nazi Germany during the war, from Argentina and take him back to Israel. He is put on trial in Jerusalem in 1961 and hanged for crimes against the Jewish people in May 1962.

JFK RULES

John F. Kennedy, age 43, narrowly wins the presidential election against the Republican Richard Nixon and becomes the 35th U.S. President.

SPY IN THE SKY

A U.S. U-2 spy plane flown by Gary Powers is shot down over Russia. The four-power summit taking place in Paris, called to reduce tension in Europe, collapses with no agreement as the United States refuses to apologize for flying over Soviet airspace.

BRASILIA BUILDINGS

Lúcio Costa and Oscar Niemeyer are the architects of the parliament buildings in Brasilia, Brazil's new capital city. The striking modernist forms of the buildings bring Latin American architecture to international prominence.

DIVIDED BUT INDEPENDENT

After five years of conflict, the island of Cyprus becomes an independent republic in the Commonwealth with the Greek Cypriot Archbishop Makarios as president and the Turkish Cypriot Dr. Fazil Kütchük as vice president.

THE BIRTH OF OPEC

In Baghdad, five oil exporting nations, Iraq, Iran, Kuwait, Saudi Arabia, and Venezuela, agree to set up the Organization of Petroleum Exporting Countries (OPEC) to protect their interests.

LA DOLCE VITA

Federico Fellini's film, starring Marcello Mastroianni, depicts and criticizes the decadent, pleasure-seeking society of Rome's "beautiful people."

ABOVE: The Voice of America broadcasts to West Berlin, offering a forum for defectors.

THE CARETAKER

The play *The Caretaker* establishes Harold Pinter as one of Britain's leading young dramatists. He is renowned for his powerful dialogue (realistic in its use of everyday language and telling pauses) and for his ability to evoke menace, stressed relationships, and mental disintegration.

THE FIRST LASER

U.S. physicist Theodore H. Maiman builds the first laser. The name comes from the initial letters of Light Amplification by Stimulated Emission of Radiation. He uses an artificial ruby cylinder to produce a beam of light that hardly spreads at all. Laser light will go on to become essential in many applications, from surgery to nightclubs.

RABBIT, RUN

This is the first of American novelist John Updike's series of novels featuring the life of ex-basketball champion Harry Angstrom. The novel, with its vivid prose, establishes Updike as a major writer.

ALBERT CAMUS
(1913–1960)

Algerian-born French existentialist novelist and former Resistance worker Albert Camus has died in a car crash, with an unfinished autobiographical novel at his side. His first novel, *The Outsider* (1942), gained him instant fame and was quickly followed by *The Myth of Sisyphus* (also 1942). Other work includes *The Plague* (1947) and *The Fall* (1956), political writings such as *Chronicles of Today* (1950–53), and a number of plays. He was also editor, with Jean-Paul Sartre, of the left-wing newspaper *Combat* in the years immediately following the liberation.

BORIS LEONIDOVICH PASTERNAK
(1890–1960)

Russian writer and poet Boris Pasternak has died. He is best known in the West for his novel *Dr. Zhivago* (1957), which portrays the disillusion that displaced the idealistic visions of the revolution. The book was banned in his own country. It is perhaps less well-known that he was for many years Russia's official translator of works by Shakespeare, Goethe, the French poet Verlaine, and other writers.

TO KILL A MOCKINGBIRD

Harper Lee's southern tale is told from the viewpoint of the two children of a white lawyer who is defending a black man unjustly accused of rape. The book will become a bestseller.

INTEGRATED CIRCUITS

Transistors become so small that they can be etched on to thin chips of silicon, producing integrated circuits; each chip can do the work of many transistors.

ROUND THE WORLD UNDER THE SEA

USS *Triton*, a nuclear submarine, becomes the first vessel to circumnavigate the Earth without ever surfacing. It completes the journey in 84 days.

DEALING WITH DELINQUENCY

In *Growing Up Absurd*, American writer and psychologist Paul Goodman draws on literature, political theory, and psychology to argue for an anti-authoritarian approach to dealing with delinquents and young offenders.

THE CHATTERLEY TRIAL

Penguin Books Limited are prosecuted for publishing "an obscene book entitled *Lady Chatterley's Lover*," the notorious book written by English novelist D.H. Lawrence, first published privately in Florence in 1928. The defense calls numerous eminent literary people who testify as to the novel's literary merit, and the publishers are cleared; the book is made legally available.

SEAFLOOR SPREADING

Harry Hammond Hess, professor of geophysics at Princeton University, puts forward the idea that the seafloor is spreading outward from the volcanic mid-ocean ridges, thus causing continental drift.

WEATHER SATELLITES

Tiros I, the first weather satellite, is launched by the United States on April 1, followed by *Tiros II* in November. What they detect greatly helps weather forecasting, especially the early detection of tornadoes and hurricanes.

MORE ACCURATE METER

The meter, originally set by Napoleon's advisors as one ten-millionth of the distance from the Equator to the North Pole, is more accurately defined as 1,650,763.73 wavelengths of orange-red light from the isotope krypton-86.

ARTIFICIAL HIPS

English surgeon John Charnley fits patients with the first artificial hip joints.

RECORD DEEP-SEA DIVE

The bathyscaphe *Trieste* descends nearly 7 miles into the Marianas Trench in the Pacific, the greatest known ocean depth. It is piloted by U.S. naval lieutenant Don Walsh and French engineer Jacques Piccard, son of its inventor, Swiss-born Belgian physicist Auguste. Piccard piloted his first bathyscaphe, an observation capsule suspended beneath a flotation tank, in 1948.

SRI LANKA'S FIRST LADY

Sirimavo Bandaranaike, widow of the assassinated prime minister of Ceylon and leader of the Sri Lanka Freedom Party, becomes the world's first woman prime minister, vowing to continue her husband's socialist policies.

ARRIVAL OF THE PILL

The first oral contraceptive, an estrogen-progesterone compound, becomes commercially available in the United States. Its producer, G.D. Searle of Illinois, is carrying out a trial on 50 women in Birmingham, U.K., preparing to introduce "the Pill" to Britain in 1961.

LIFE WITH THE LIONS

Born Free, an account of her work with lions in Kenya, by German-born writer Joy Adamson, is widely influential in publicizing the increasing threat to the world's wild animals.

WINTER OLYMPICS

The Eighth Winter Games in California take place in a resort built from scratch for them at Squaw Valley. Hosts America win the ice hockey gold against expectations and the Scandinavian's hold on the Nordic events is broken by two German winners.

SOCCER RECORD

Spanish team Real Madrid take soccer's European Cup for the fifth consecutive time with a thrilling 7–3 triumph over Eintracht Frankfurt in the final. Ferenc Puskas scores four goals and Alfredo Di Stefano adds a hat trick.

DEPLETING THE SEAS

The world fisheries catch for 1960 reaches 40 million tons, double that of 1950. Soviet trawlers and purse seiners reduce herring populations along the U.S. Atlantic coast by 90 percent and virtually wipe out haddock.

ABOVE: The U.S. Army's new Pershing missile, a two-stage ballistic weapon, on a test launch from a portable transporter-erector.

OLYMPICS AT ROME

The Soviets lead foes America in the medal table at the 17th Olympiad in Rome. At his sixth Games, Hungarian Aladar Gerevich ends his career at age 50 by adding a fencing gold to his collection of six golds, a silver, and a bronze. Cassius Clay (later Muhammad Ali) takes the gold medal for light-heavyweight boxing and Wilma Rudolph wins three golds in the sprinting events.

A NEW PEN

The first felt tip pen, the August Pentel, is introduced by the Tokyo Stationery Co.

BELOW: The shambles left by the worst of a series of earthquakes to hit Chile this year.

RUNNING THE SPACE RACE

There is crisis in Cuba after a botched U.S.-backed invasion. The United States sends a large number of military observers to Vietnam, taking the first step on a path paved with good intentions that will lead to all-out conflict. The big story of the year is the race to put a man in space, which is won by the Russians as cosmonaut Yuri Gagarin orbits the Earth in triumph. American Alan B. Shepard gets there second in a spacecraft that can be controlled by its pilot.

BELOW: The Moon becomes the focus for the rivalry between the United States and the U.S.S.R.

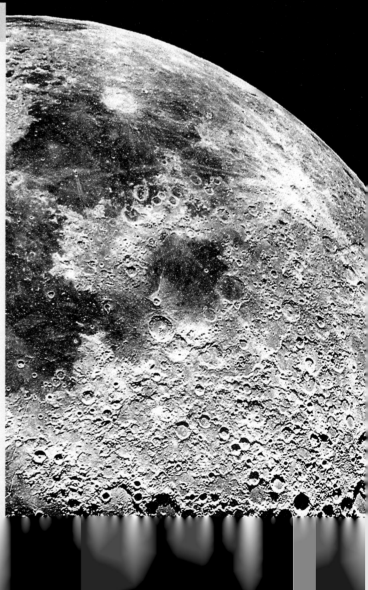

1961

Jan	14	South Africa introduces new decimal currency
	20	John F. Kennedy is inaugurated as U.S. President
Apr	12	Soviet cosmonaut Yuri Gagarin becomes the first man in space
	17	Cuban exiles land at the Bay of Pigs, Cuba, but are routed
May	5	U.S. astronaut Alan B. Shepard becomes the second man in space
	31	South Africa leaves the Commonwealth as an independent republic
Aug	13	East Germans build the Berlin Wall to separate East and West Berlin
Sep	17	U.N. Secretary General Dag Hammarskjöld is killed in a plane crash over the Congo

BAY OF PIGS INCIDENT
In April, 1,500 Cuban exiles, trained by U.S. military instructors, land in the Bay of Pigs (Bahia de Cochinos) in Cuba. The expected revolt against Fidel Castro fails to materialize and the invaders are killed or captured. The U.S. government faces considerable criticism for its action.

ALGERIAN COUP FAILS
The French Army revolts against de Gaulle's government over its policy for independence in Algeria. De Gaulle declares a state of emergency and the coup collapses. The rebel leaders are tried for treason and eight are sentenced to death.

TOP LEFT AND RIGHT: Automobiles begin to take over; production rises and road systems become more complicated.

ABOVE: Cuban leader Fidel Castro plans battle strategy on the run during the Bay of Pigs invasion by the United States.

RIGHT: Cuban troops launch a counterattack at Playa Larga.

INDEPENDENCE IN AFRICA

Sierra Leone (in May) and Tanganyika (in December) both gain independence from British rule.

THE WALL GOES UP

The East German authorities seal off West Berlin and erect a wall across the city, thus preventing the escape of East Germans to the West.

BABI YAR

The poem by Russian poet Yevgeny Yevtushenko (b. 1933) commemorates Jews massacred at Babi Yar, near Kiev, during World War II. His stand is against Soviet as well as Nazi anti-Semitism.

TRAGEDY FOR U.N.

U.N. Secretary General Dag Hammarskjöld is killed in a plane crash while trying to obtain peace in the Congo. His successor at the helm of the U.N. is a Burmese diplomat, U Thant.

A DANCER DEFECTS

Touring with the Kirov Ballet, Russian dancer Rudolf Nureyev (1938–1993) leaps to freedom over an airport barrier while the company is in Paris. His defection brings a new star to Western ballet, and brings dance into the news. From 1962 on, he will regularly dance with partner Margot Fonteyn.

MORE MILITARY HELP

The United States increases the number of military advisers in South Vietnam to defend the government against Communist incursions from the north.

CATCH 22

American writer Joseph Heller's huge first novel, about life in the American Air Force during World War II, enjoys great commercial success. The title, *Catch 22*, adds a new phrase to the language. The book hits out at bureaucracy as well as war.

A NEW CONTRACEPTIVE

The loop, an IUD (intrauterine device) contraceptive, is introduced by an American, Jack Lippes. Made of inert plastic, it is less likely to irritate the body or to be rejected than Ernest Grafenburg's simple silver ring, introduced in the 1930s.

FIRST MAN IN SPACE

The Soviet Union beats the United States to win the space race. On April 12, cosmonaut Yuri Gagarin (1934–68) of the Soviet Union becomes the first man to orbit the Earth in a spacecraft launched from aboard *Vostok 1* from Kazakhstan. He completes a single orbit of the Earth at a maximum altitude of 204 miles and a maximum speed of 1,746 miles per hour. His craft parachutes down safely after 88 minutes near the village of Smelovka in Saratov, U.S.S.R.

FIRST AMERICAN IN SPACE

On May 5, astronaut Alan Bartlett Shepard, Jr., of the United States makes the world's second space flight, a "hop" of just 15 minutes in the *Freedom 7* capsule.

SECOND RUSSIAN IN SPACE

On August 6, cosmonaut Gherman Titov of the Soviet Union makes 17 orbits of the Earth, a day-long space flight.

MOON PLEDGE

On May 25, U.S. president John F. Kennedy says the United States will aim to put the first man on the Moon.

THE HUNTING OF THE QUARK

American theoretical physicist Murray Gell-Mann introduces the quark theory to account for the strange behavior of particles. It will win him the Nobel Prize for Physics in 1969.

MEGACITY

In December, Tokyo becomes the world's first city to have a population of ten million.

ERNEST MILLAR HEMINGWAY
(1899–1961)

The American writer and Nobel Prize winner has died by his own hand at his home in Idaho from a bullet in the mouth. After World War I (in which he worked as an ambulance driver for the Red Cross), he returned to journalism as a roving correspondent in Paris and began his career as a hard-living, hard-drinking, and later bull-fighting, writer. He was four times married and lived in Europe and Florida before settling in Cuba. Among his best-known works are *The Sun Also Rises* (1926), *A Farewell to Arms* (1929), *Death In the Afternoon* (1932), *For Whom the Bell Tolls* (1940, about the Spanish Civil War) and *The Old Man and the Sea* (1952).

ATMOSPHERES

Hungarian composer György Ligeti creates *Atmosphères*, a shimmering orchestral work in which every musician plays a separate part, the whole weaving together to create a floating, atmospheric texture. Ligeti himself describes it as one of his most radical works.

BEATING THE BABE

Roger Maris passes the supposedly unbreakable record of fellow Yankee, Babe Ruth, by hitting his 61st home run of the year. Maris has the advantage of a longer baseball season but the media attention is intense and the stress is so great that his hair starts to fall out.

BATTLE OF THE BULGE

Weight Watchers is founded by American housewife Jean Nidetch. Her weight-loss program combines a high-protein diet (devised by Norman Joliffe of the New York Department of Health) with the proscription of certain foods and the use of group therapy methods.

LAWRENCIUM CREATED

The artificially created element 103, lawrencium, is synthesized by four U.S. scientists, Albert Ghiorso, Torbjørn Sikkeland, Almon E. Larsh, and Robert M. Latimer. It is named after Ernest Lawrence, the American inventor of the cyclotron.

GOLF BALL TYPEWRITER

International Business Machines introduces the "golf ball" typewriter. The characters are mounted on a rotating sphere instead of on separate type bars. The typeface can be changed by changing the golf ball.

STREET FIGHTING MEN

In the Netherlands, youth groups, or the *nozems* (rowdies), clash with police on the streets of The Hague, marking the beginning of the 1960s youth protest movements in Europe.

EXPANDING CAMPUSES

Three new universities are to be built in Britain, marking the start of a huge worldwide expansion in university education, designed to accommodate the postwar baby boom.

FREEDOM FIGHTERS

Amnesty International, a nonpolitical organization to help prisoners of conscience anywhere in the world, is founded in Britain.

TIME TO CHANGE

Electronic watches are introduced to the market. Winding becomes a thing of the past as the watches are battery driven.

BELOW: Oil derricks at Baytown, Texas. The oil from these rigs is used to make gasoline for the growing number of automobiles.

ABOVE: Number 57 begins to flip after losing a wheel in the Daytona 500 race held at Daytona International Speedway, Daytona Beach, Florida.

AIR TRAGEDY

Eighteen members of the United States figure skating club were killed while in route to the world championships being held in Prague when the plane they and 54 others were riding crashed near Brussels.

SAVING THE ANIMALS

The World Wildlife Fund, an international organization to raise funds for wildlife conservation by public appeal, is founded. Its headquarters are in Switzerland. It will later become the World Wide Fund for Nature.

PATRICE LUMUMBA
(1925–1961)

Patrice Lumumba (born Katako Kombe), who became the first prime minister of the Democratic Republic of the Congo when the country gained independence from Belgium last year, has been arrested by his own army and murdered by the Katangese.

CARL GUSTAV JUNG
(1875–1961)

Carl Jung, the Swiss psychiatrist who has given us the concepts of the collective unconscious, introvert and extrovert, and the school of analytical psychology, has died. Early in the century, Jung worked in Vienna with Sigmund Freud, but they parted company over the latter's overinsistence (in Jung's view) on the psychosexual nature of neurosis. Among Jung's works are *The Psychology of the Unconscious* (1911–1912), *Psychology and Religion* (1937), and *The Undiscovered Self* (1957). He had just completed his autobiography, *Memories, Dreams, Reflections*, to be published in 1962.

THE END OF COLONIALISM IN INDIA

Indian forces invade Portuguese Goa and other enclaves in India, removing the last European colonies.

BELOW: Missiles being transported to Cuba soon trigger the Cuban Missile Crisis.

FIRST AMERICAN IN SPACE

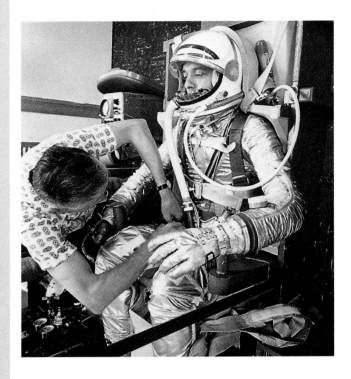

ABOVE: Astronaut Alan Shepard suits up for his space trip.

BELOW: Safe splashdown and rescue from the Atlantic.

BELOW: The president congratulates America's first space hero.

ABOVE: *Freedom 7* blasts off from Cape Canaveral.

THE WORLD ON THE BRINK

The Soviet Union and the United States confront each other in Cuba and the world holds its breath as nuclear war seems to be imminent. Diplomacy saves the day. The space race continues. U.S. astronaut John Glenn orbits the Earth three times and *Telstar*, the first communications satellite, is launched into permanent orbit and so catches the public imagination that a song is written for it. An unmanned space probe, complete with camera, is dispatched to photograph the planet Venus. James Bond, super spy, makes his first appearance on the world's cinema screen and beautiful Marilyn Monroe is found dead.

1962

Jan	1	Western Samoa becomes the first independent Pacific state
Feb	20	Astronaut John Glenn makes the first true U.S. space flight with three orbits of the Earth
Mar	2	Wilt Chamberlain is the first man to score 100 points in a professional basketball game
July	3	Algeria wins independence from France
	10	*Telstar*, first telecommunications satellite, is launched
Aug	5	Marilyn Monroe, American glamour star, is found dead
Sep	30	The University of Mississippi admits its first black student and riots ensue
Oct	9	Uganda becomes independent within the Commonwealth
	22	U.S. president John F. Kennedy announces that the Soviet Union has established missile bases in Cuba
Nov	10	World renown physicist Niels Bohr dies in Copenhagen at the age of 77
Dec	10	John Steinbeck receives the Nobel Prize for literature
	14	Space probe *Mariner 2* makes the first flight to another planet, passing close to Venus

LEFT: A U.S. sentry keeps watch during the Cuban crisis.

MORE INDEPENDENCE

Western Samoa becomes the first Pacific island state to gain its independence from Britain. During the year, Jamaica, Trinidad and Tobago, and Uganda all become independent from Britain. Burundi and Rwanda gain their independence from Belgium.

LAWRENCE OF ARABIA

British director David Lean's sprawling epic brings together all the elements of film — camerawork, acting, settings, music, and so on — to make a notable whole, one of the masterpieces of British cinema. The film also makes Peter O'Toole an international star and introduces Omar Sharif to American audiences.

TWA BUILDING, KENNEDY AIRPORT

Finnish-born architect Eero Saarinen (1910–1961) designed the dramatic shell-concrete roof of the terminal, which is completed this year. It reminds many observers of a soaring bird. Although the architect denied that this was what he had in mind, the building shows that, for many, modern architecture can hold symbolic meanings.

TELSTAR LAUNCHED

America launches the first telecommunications satellite, *Telstar 1*. It makes possible transatlantic TV pictures, but only in 20 minute sessions. This marks the beginning of global telecommunications.

CUBAN CRISIS

After the Soviet Union places nuclear missiles in Cuba, the United States blockades the island. The United States and Soviet Union confront each other, bringing the world to the brink of nuclear warfare, before the Soviet missiles are removed.

ABOVE: Costa Rican students protest against the Soviet Union's intervention in Cuba.

LEFT: Marilyn Monroe, who dies this year, is shown entertaining the troops.

MARILYN MONROE (NORMA JEAN MORTENSON) (1926–1962)

American movie star Marilyn Monroe is found dead, apparently after taking an overdose of sleeping pills. After working as a model and bit-part Hollywood actress, she made her name with *How to Marry a Millionaire* and *Gentlemen Prefer Blondes* (both 1953) and went on to make the comedies *The Seven-Year Itch* (1955) and *Some Like it Hot* (1959). She then took acting lessons at the Actor's Studio and married playwright Arthur Miller, who wrote *The Misfits* (1961) for her, and from whom she was divorced last year. Her name has been linked with those of both the president of the United States, John F. Kennedy, and his brother Robert.

ABOVE: *Telstar* is assembled in Bell Telephone Laboratories. The signals it sends from space will be picked up by the tracker (below).

FIRST TRUE U.S. SPACE FLIGHT

U.S. astronaut John Glenn, Jr., makes America's first true space flight, three orbits of the Earth in the spacecraft *Friendship 7*. He remains in space for five hours.

TWO CHEESEBURGERS WITH EVERYTHING

American sculptor Claes Oldenburg, one of the leaders of the pop art movement, is famed for his off-beat, surreal interpretations of everyday items (plaster models magnified many times). Now he turns to soft sculpture, in which a subject is modeled in soft materials and stuffed with kapok. *Soft Typewriter* (1963) and *Soft Toilet* (1966) will follow.

DR. NO

The first in the series of movies featuring British agent James Bond, based on the creation of novelist Ian Fleming, is made. This one stars Scottish actor Sean Connery, who becomes identified with the part and will star in six further Bond films.

TAPE CASSETTES

Dutch electronics firm Philips introduces the compact tape recorder cassette. These can be played on portable tape machines. This will lead to music cassettes and talking newspapers for the blind.

ONE DAY IN THE LIFE OF IVAN DENISOVICH

Russian novelist Alexander Solzhenitsyn's novel of the Soviet Gulag describes the prisoner's world in the most vivid terms. For many in the West, it is the first such account to reach them.

THALIDOMIDE TRAGEDY

Thalidomide, introduced in 1958 as a safe sleeping tablet and remedy for morning sickness during pregnancy, is withdrawn after it is found that some women who take it give birth to children with serious abnormalities.

MARINER 2 LAUNCHED

U.S. space probe *Mariner 2* sets out on a voyage to inspect Venus, the first such trip to another planet. It measures the planet's temperature and confirms the existence of solar wind.

VIVE ALGERIE

After eight years of warfare, Algeria wins its independence from France. Ben Bella becomes president of the new republic.

EQUAL EDUCATION

Black student and Air Force veteran James Howard Meredith enrolls at the University of Mississippi, which is ordered to admit him by a court order upheld by the Supreme Court. Governor Ross Barnett, in a telephone conversation with President Kennedy, refused to concede and promised to sustain school segregation. Rioting breaks out on campus when he makes his first attempt to enter on September 30 and he is escorted by federal marshals and troops.

SILENT SPRING

American marine biologist Rachel Carson writes this chastening book warning of the indiscriminate use of pesticides. Her success in alarming the public begins a new era in environmental awareness.

BEER IN CANS

Beer is marketed in aluminum cans that open with pull-off tabs by the Aluminum Corporation of America. First produced in 1958, aluminum cans replace the traditional steel can plated with tin.

THE BERLIN WALL GOES UP

LEFT: East Berliners carry red flags on the first May Day parade after the Wall goes up.

BELOW LEFT: Willy Brandt, the mayor of West Berlin, and his sons look at the Soviet sector.

BELOW: East Berlin troops display military might and weaponry, although a number of soldiers defect to the West.

BOTTOM: President Kennedy visits the Berlin Wall.

A DREAM AND AN ASSASSINATION

Valentina Tereshkova scores a first for Russia and for women as she becomes the first female astronaut. A hotline telephone link is established between the White House and the Kremlin. President de Gaulle keeps the U.K. out of the EEC. Indonesia and Malaya seize independence, and African nations unite under the umbrella of the Organization of African Unity. Black civil rights leader Martin Luther King leads a march on Washington, D.C. and delivers a speech that will become famous. The year ends in tragedy and shock as President Kennedy is assassinated.

1963

Jan	29	American poet Robert Frost dies at age 88
	29	The European Economic Community rejects Britain's request to join
June	3	Pope John XXIII dies after four years in office
	16	First woman in space, U.S.S.R.'s Valentina Tereshkova, begins her three day flight
	20	The United States and U.S.S.R. agree to set up a "hotline" between the White House in Washington, D.C. and the Kremlin in Moscow
	26	President Kennedy delivers his famous speech at the Berlin Wall
July	31	In Britain, the Peerage Act allows hereditary peers to disclaim their titles; Viscount Stansgate (Tony Benn) is the first
Aug	5	The United States, Soviet Union, and Britain sign the Nuclear Test-Ban Treaty
	28	Black leader Martin Luther King, Jr. makes his "I have a dream" speech in Washington, D.C.
Sep	15	Confrontation begins between Malaysia and Indonesia
Oct	18	U.K. premier Harold Macmillan resigns; he is succeeded by the earl of Home (who will later renounce his title)
Nov	22	President John F. Kennedy is assassinated in Dallas; he is succeeded by Vice President Lyndon B. Johnson
	24	Jack Ruby kills Lee Harvey Oswald, who had been accused of Kennedy's murder

ABOVE: The Texas School Book Depository, allegedly the place from which President Kennedy was shot. Possible positions for the killer are marked.

RIGHT: Alleged killer Lee Harvey Oswald in custody for the murder of the president. Before he can stand trial he is shot dead by Jack Ruby.

INDEPENDENCE FOR THE EAST INDIES

The final Dutch East Indies colony, West Irian, becomes part of Indonesia. In September, the British colonies of Singapore, Sarawak, and Sabah join Malaya in the Federation of Malaysia. Conflict begins as Indonesian forces infiltrate Malaysia in an attempt to gain control over the whole of Borneo. British, Commonwealth, and Malaysian forces counterattack. The Commonwealth military and civilian services suffered 150 dead and 234 wounded, with four captured; the Indonesians count 590 dead, 222 wounded, and 771 captured. Conflict continues until a peace agreement is finally signed in August 1966.

AFRICA UNITES

The Organization of African Unity (OAU) is formed in Addis Ababa, the Ethiopian capital, by African leaders to increase cooperation and remove colonialism from the continent.

KENNEDY IN BERLIN

President Kennedy visits West Berlin to support freedom, stating that "Ich bin ein Berliner" (I am a Berliner). In the same month, a "hotline" telephone link is established between Washington, D.C. and Moscow.

BANNING THE BOMB

Britain, the United States, and the Soviet Union sign the Nuclear Test-Ban Treaty, prohibiting weapon tests in outer space, the atmosphere, and under water. Many other nations sign the treaty later.

I HAVE A DREAM

More than 200,000 civil rights protesters, led by Martin Luther King, Jr., march in Washington, D.C. In his "I have a dream" speech, King states that one day African-Americans will gain true equality.

DEATH IN TEXAS

President Kennedy is assassinated in Dallas, apparently by a lone gunman. Vice President Lyndon B. Johnson takes over. A loner named Lee Harvey Oswald is quickly arrested but is assassinated before he gets to trial. The Kennedy assassination will engender countless conspiracy theories for the rest of the century.

FIRST WOMAN IN SPACE

Russian cosmonaut Valentina Tereshkova becomes the first woman in space when she makes 45 orbits of the Earth piloting *Vostok 6*.

QUASARS IDENTIFIED

Quasars, Quasi-Stellar Objects, are identified by American astronomer Allan Rex Sandage and the Australian astronomer Cyril Hazard. Quasars are objects in deep space, possibly galaxies, that may be as far as 16 billion light years away.

ENTER THE MOUSE

U.S. scientist Douglas Engelbart invents the computer mouse, a device for controlling an on-screen pointer.

ABOVE: Joan Baez and Bob Dylan, princess and prince of the protest song, at the civil rights demonstration led by Martin Luther King, Jr.

DUTCH PROTEST

In the Netherlands, the Provos (young "provocateurs") campaign vigorously for the liberation of repressed minority groups such as homosexuals, the introduction of antipollution laws, and the preservation of inner-city areas from property development.

SCORPIO RISING

Kenneth Anger, doyen of underground independent filmmaking, makes *Scorpio Rising*, a documentary about motorcyclists in New York. Although made outside the normal film creation and distribution channels, it will be seen by millions of viewers over the years.

NEW ALLIANCES IN AFRICA

Kenya and Zanzibar become independent nations in the British Commonwealth. Zanzibar joins with Tanganyika to form the new nation of Tanzania, in April 1964.

LEDS INVENTED

U.S. scientist Nick Holonyak invents the Light-Emitting Diode (LED), a semiconductor device that glows when a current passes through it; they are used for clocks, calculators, and other display lights.

CARBON FIBER

Engineers at England's Royal Aircraft Establishment invent carbon fiber. It is a thin, tough fiber of nearly pure carbon combined with plastics. It is used in spacecraft because it is light, yet very strong.

FIRST HOLOGRAPHS

U.S. scientists Emmett Leith and Juris Upatneiks give the first demonstration of holography, using the recently invented laser to project light to form three-dimensional images.

DE GAULLE A DIT NON

General de Gaulle forcefully vetoes Great Britain's attempt to join the European Economic Community.

THE FEMININE MYSTIQUE

Betty Friedan publishes *The Feminine Mystique*, a study of the social conditioning that shapes women's lives. She argues that women are victimized by false values and delusions that lead them to find fulfillment in husbands and children.

BUNKER MENTALITY

Nuclear bomb shelters are built in the cellars of houses and other private buildings across the United States and stocked with the necessities of life by citizens fearful of a nuclear war.

FLOATING BLADES

The Hover lawnmower is produced by Flymo, a British company. It works on the same principle as the hovercraft, which floats on a cushion of air just above the ground, so it is easy to push across grassy gardens.

DEATHS IN THE FRENCH ARTS

Poet and writer Jean Cocteau, composer François Poulenc, and artist Georges Braque all die this year.

OPPOSITE: President Kennedy's family at his funeral in Washington, D.C.

EDITH PIAF
(EDITH GIOVANNA GASSION)
(1915–1963)

French chanteuse Edith Piaf has died after a long period of illness. The "little sparrow" whose father was a well-known acrobat and who began her career singing in the streets of Paris, became famous for songs such as "La Vie en Rose" and "Non, je ne regrette rien."

ABOVE: Refugees from Cuba adrift off the coast of Miami.

ABOVE: Engineers work on a Mariner spacecraft at Cape Canaveral, fixing solar panels to harness the power of the Sun.

BLACK CIVIL RIGHTS MOVEMENT

ABOVE: The charismatic Martin Luther King, Jr., leads the march.

ABOVE: Many black celebrities such as actor Sidney Poiter and singer Harry Belafonte join the protest.

BELOW: What started as a peaceful demonstration turns to violence as protesters make the strength of their feelings known.

BELOW: Entertainer Sammy Davis, Jr., joins the cause.

OPPOSITE: The 20,000 marchers reach the Mall in Washington, D.C.

ABOVE: Tension between white and black youths can be felt on the streets.

THE SIXTIES START TO SWING

Tension rises in southern Africa as Nelson Mandela, leader of the African National Congress, is jailed for life in South Africa and Ian Smith plans a unilateral declaration of independence on behalf of the whites in Southern Rhodesia. Things are looking better in the United States, when Martin Luther King, Jr., receives the Nobel Peace Prize and the Civil Rights Act becomes law. Three Russian cosmonauts orbit the Earth together and the U.S. probe *Ranger* takes the first photographs of the Moon's hidden dark side.

1 9 6 4

Jan	29	Ninth Winter Olympics open at Innsbruck, Austria
Apr	5	U.S. General Douglas MacArthur dies at age 84
	12	Arnold Palmer led all challengers the entire four rounds to win a record fourth Masters Championship in Augusta, Georgia
May	27	India's Prime Minister Jawaharlal Nehru dies at age 74
June	14	In South Africa, African National Congress leader Nelson Mandela is jailed for life for trying to overthrow the government
July	2	President Johnson signs the Civil Rights Act of 1964 into law prohibiting racial discrimination
July	6	British territory Nyasaland becomes independent as Malawi
	31	Space probe *Ranger* photographs the Moon
Oct	10	Eighteenth Olympic Games open in Tokyo
	12	First three-man space flight by Soviet crew
	14	Martin Luther King, Jr. is awarded the Nobel Peace Prize
	15	Soviet leader Nikita Khrushchev is deposed. He is replaced by Leonid Brezhnev and Alexei Kosygin
	16	Harold Wilson forms Labour government in Britain
	24	Northern Rhodesia becomes independent as Zambia
Nov	3	President Lyndon Johnson defeats Barry Goldwater in a landslide

LEFT: British pop combo the Beatles take America by storm. Their fans (above) display all the symptoms of Beatlemania.

MANDELA JAILED

Nelson Mandela, leader of the African National Congress, is sentenced to life imprisonment for sabotage and attempting to overthrow the government after the Rivona trial. He is sent to Robben Island in Table Bay, Cape Town, South Africa.

MORE FREEDOM FOR AFRICA

In October, both Malawi and Northern Rhodesia (now known as Zambia), gain their independence from Britain, thus ending the British attempt to construct a Central African Federation. Only white-dominated southern Africa, plus a few small British, Spanish, and Portuguese colonies in West Africa, still remain in European hands.

AMERICAN CIVIL RIGHTS

The Civil Rights Act becomes law in the United States. It prohibits racial discrimination in employment, public accommodation, union membership, and federally funded programs. The act is the biggest single civil rights law in U.S. history.

KHRUSHCHEV OUSTED

Russian premier Nikita Khrushchev is deposed while on holiday at his country *dacha* and replaced by Leonid Brezhnev as Communist party leader. Alexei Kosygin is named the prime minister.

HOUSE FOR VANNA VENTURI

American architect Robert Venturi designs a proto-postmodern house for his mother in Chestnut Hill, Pennsylvania. Numerous features of the building (for example, the broken line of the entrance facade) look forward to the postmodern style, reflecting the fact that Venturi was writing his book, *Complexity and Contradiction in Architecture*, while the house was being built. This and his other writings argue for the importance of historical links and the inspiration of popular culture in architecture.

MARAT/SADE

The Persecution and Assassination of Marat as Performed by the Inmates of the Asylum of Charenton under the Direction of the Marquis de Sade (aka *Marat/Sade*) will be Peter Weiss's most famous play. It becomes the archetype of the Theater of Cruelty. In it, Sade directs his play depicting the murder of Marat while lunatics murmur in the background.

FOR THE UNION DEAD

In this and other volumes, American poet Robert Lowell stands up against the deadening, depersonalizing influence of war and violence. His concern for America and its traditions sets him apart from his contemporary "confessional" poets and marks him out as perhaps America's most powerful living poet.

ABOVE: Black voters exercise their rights in Baton Rouge.

BELOW: Brazilians celebrate a successful revolution in Rio.

MR. SMITH TAKES CHARGE

Ian Smith becomes prime minister of Southern Rhodesia. He disagrees with the British plan to give democratic rights to the African majority and declares unilateral independence (UDI).

DEATHS IN THE ENTERTAINMENT WORLD

Silent brother Adolph "Harpo" Marx (b. 1884) dies, as does writer Ian Fleming (b. 1908), the creator of James Bond. Irish playwrights Brendan Behan (b. 1925) and Sean O'Casey (b. 1884) also die.

DR. STRANGELOVE, OR HOW I LEARNED TO STOP WORRYING AND LOVE THE BOMB

Stanley Kubrick (1928–1999) directs this antiwar comedy, which stars Peter Sellers in three roles. It becomes popular all over a world that is sensitized to the nuclear question by the recent Cuban Missile Crisis.

REQUIEM

Russian poet Anna Akhmatova's elegiac tribute to those who perished under Stalin is published, after being suppressed since Akhmatova wrote it in the 1940s. Its appearance confirms her status as Russia's greatest and most courageous twentieth century poet.

FAB FOUR IN AMERICA

English pop group the Beatles, already legends in their own land, conquer America. Beatlemania grips American teenagers.

SHOT RED MARILYN

Andy Warhol produces one of his most famous pop art images, in which subject matter from popular culture is depicted. The modern reproduction method of using the silkscreen technique, which Warhol was one of the first to exploit, is utilized.

JAWAHARLAL (PANDIT) NEHRU (1889–1964)

The Harrow and Cambridge educated Indian leader and statesman Jawaharlal Nehru, known as Pandit or "teacher," has died. He spent a total of 18 years in prison under British rule, during which time he was elected president of the Indian National Congress (1928). He became the first prime minister of India in 1947, was responsible for India's nonalignment policy and the development of an industrial base.

IN C
American composer Terry Riley is one of the originators of minimalism and this piece brings the movement fame. The work consists of a repeated high C on the piano, which forms a backdrop to a series of 53 short fragments, which the players may repeat any number of times (but they have to do all 53 in a set order). There can be any number of players.

BULLET TRAIN
Japan's "Bullet Train" service between Tokyo and Osaka begins, with speeds up to 125 miles per hour.

MULTIPERSON SPACE FLIGHT
In October, the Soviet spacecraft *Voshkod I* carries three cosmonauts on a 16-orbit mission, the first multiperson space flight.

BELOW: Finnish troops serving with the U.N. force help to keep the peace during unrest on the island of Cyprus.

ABOVE: Funded by the U.S. AID program, the first stages of the Sharavathi Hydroelectric Project near Mysore, India, approach completion.

BELOW: The Cleveland Browns battle with the Baltimore Colts for the 1964 NFL title game. Jim Brown helps Cleveland to win the championship.

ABOVE: The cameras used on board the unmanned *Ranger II* spacecraft send back over 4,000 pictures of the cosmos.

ABOVE: Brigitte Bardot, international sex symbol and actress, is later to champion animal welfare rights and the cause of endangered species.

ELEMENT 104

Scientists in Russia and the United States both claim to have artificially created element 104; the names kurchatovium, rutherfordium, and unnilquadium are all proposed for it.

BOYS' TOYS

A toy soldier doll aimed at boys, named Action Man in Europe and G.I. Joe in the United States, is launched by Hasbro. It is as big a hit as Barbie has been with the girls. Combat accessories and a wardrobe of uniforms are also provided.

BELOW: The Warren Commission is set up to investigate the Kennedy assassination. Its findings will not satisfy everybody.

ENGLAND SWINGS

Time magazine announces Swinging London, where a consumer boom rages. Clothes designed to outrage are sold in diminutive boutiques instead of department stores or couture houses. Discothèques are new-style nightclubs with lights flashing in time to amplified pop music, and homes are being transformed by designer Terence Conran's style ideas at Habitat, his furniture and interiors shop.

DISASTER IN ALASKA

An earthquake in Alaska measuring 8.4 on the Richter scale (later upgraded to 9.2) kills 110 people and sets off a 220 foot *tsunami* (tidal wave), the largest ever recorded.

ABOVE: The Unisphere, symbol of the New York World's Fair. Over 200,000 people visit on the first Sunday of its opening.

BACKGROUND RADIATION
American scientists Arno Allen Prenzias and Robert Woodrow Wilson discover background microwave radiation coming from all directions in space; it is thought to be an "echo" of the Big Bang with which it is believed that the universe started.

DARK GLASSES
Photochromic spectacles are invented by Dr. Stookey at the Corning Glass Works, New York. They are made from silica glass embedded with silver compound crystals. These absorb light, so the glasses darken rapidly when exposed to the sun, clearing again when light levels fall.

WINTER OLYMPICS
Thousands of tons of snow are moved to Innsbruck by the Austrian Army to permit the Ninth Winter Games to take place. Eleven hundred competitors take part in 34 events; both figures are records. Soviet Lidia Skoblikova wins all four speed skating golds and Sjoukje Dijkstra wins the figure skating for Holland. Lugeing, in which athletes slide down an ice course on their backs on a toboggan, makes its Olympic debut.

MOON SHOTS
U.S. Ranger spacecraft takes the first close-up television pictures of the Moon.

HE'S THE GREATEST
Cassius Clay beats champion Sonny Liston to take the heavyweight boxing championship at age 22. Clay had embraced the Black Muslim faith in 1962 and, as champion, uses his position to challenge racism in America. He changes his name to Muhammad Ali and refuses to be drafted for the Vietnam War. For that, he is stripped of his title. He does not fight between June 1967 and February 1970, but will return to win the heavyweight crown two more times.

SOUTH AFRICAN SPORT BOYCOTT
The International Olympic Committee bans South Africa over apartheid. The international community later institutes a ban on all sporting links with South Africa.

JAPANESE OLYMPICS
The 18th Games in Tokyo, 24 years after war robbed the city of the Olympics, are the first in Asia and see many world records set. Judo and volleyball are added and athletes from a record 93 nations take part.

RIGHT: Cassius Clay, soon to be Muhammad Ali, dances like a butterfly and stings like a bee.

RACE RIOTS AND THE LITTLE RED BOOK

In the United States, Black Muslim leader Malcolm X is assassinated, Nobel Prize winner Martin Luther King, Jr. is arrested marching in Alabama, and riots flare in Watts, Los Angeles. Meanwhile, in China, the Cultural Revolution is under way, instigated by Mao Zedong and codified in his *Little Red Book*. In space, the first space walk takes place and *Mariner 4* sends back pictures of the craters on Mars. War breaks out between India and Pakistan. Britain declares Rhodesia's UDI illegal and the country plunges into conflict.

1965

Jan	24	Britain's wartime leader Sir Winston Churchill dies at age 90
Feb	1	Martin Luther King, Jr. arrested after leading civil rights march in Alabama
	21	U.S. black leader Malcolm X is assassinated in New York
Mar	18	Soviet cosmonaut Alexei Leonov performs the first space walk
Apr	6	*Early Bird*, the first geostationary telecommunications satellite, is launched
	23	Edward Murrow, CBS newsman, dies of lung cancer at the age of 53
July	14	U.S. space probe *Mariner 4* photographs Mars
Aug	15	Race riots break out in the Watts area of Los Angeles
Sep	1	War breaks out between India and Pakistan over Kashmir
	4	Franco-German missionary Albert Schweitzer dies in Africa at age 90
Nov	11	White government of Rhodesia makes illegal unilateral declaration of independence

LEFT: Malcolm X, the black American civil rights leader, is assassinated in New York.

MALCOLM X KILLED
Malcolm X, a prominent Black Muslim, is assassinated by his former colleagues in New York. Malcolm X had opposed the nonviolent civil rights movement of Martin Luther King, Jr., and supported black separatism, but in recent years, had favored cooperation rather than confrontation between the races.

MARCHING IN ALABAMA
Martin Luther King, Jr., leads a march from Selma to Montgomery in Alabama to protest against the lack of civil rights in the southern state. In August, race riots break out in the Watts district of Los Angeles as racial tension rises throughout the United States.

WAR BETWEEN INDIA AND PAKISTAN
Border clashes break out between India and Pakistan on the Kutch–Sind border in April. In September, Pakistani forces cross the cease-fire line in Kashmir, leading to war. India moves 900,000 troops into West Pakistan. In fighting near Lahore, the Pakistanis lose 450 tanks. Indian casualties are 2,212 dead, 7,636 wounded, and 1,500 missing. Pakistan estimates over 5,800 dead. Peace talks are successful at Tashkent in the Soviet Union during January 1966.

CRATERS ON MARS
The U.S. space probe *Mariner 4* photographs Mars from only 6,063 miles away and transmits 21 pictures. The photographs show that the surface is pitted with craters like the Moon but reveals no signs of life.

THE TERRACOTTA ARMY
The tomb of a Chinese Han Dynasty king, Liu Sheng, King of Zhongshan (near Beijing) 154–112 B.C., is found to contain 3,000 life-like representations of cavalry and foot soldiers. The king is covered with 2,156 jade wafers sewn together with gold thread.

ABOVE: Eero Saarinen's eagle-shaped terminal for TWA at Kennedy Airport, New York City.

CULTURAL REVOLUTION IN CHINA
Chinese leader Lin Piao urges a Cultural Revolution to renew revolutionary zeal and root out those opposed to the revolution. The Red Guards, who are leading the new revolution, target intellectuals and party officials, and many schools are shut down. The Cultural Revolution introduces the cult of Mao Zedong, and continues until the dismissal of the president, Liu Shaoqi, in October 1968.

IN THE HEAT OF THE NIGHT
Rioting erupts in Watts, a district of Los Angeles, after a black man is arrested for drunk driving.

ARIEL
American poet Sylvia Plath's most famous book of poems impresses readers with a voice in which tight verbal and poetic control is used to describe extreme situations and unstable mental states.

ALBERT SCHWEITZER
(1875–1965)

Alsace-born Franco-German missionary, musicologist, and theologian, Dr. Albert Schweitzer, has died. In 1913, having qualified as a doctor, he went with his wife to set up a medical mission in French Equatorial Africa, where leprosy and sleeping sickness were rife. He was known in Europe for the organ recitals he gave to fund his missionary project and for his many writings on religion, culture, and music. In 1952, he was awarded the Nobel Peace Prize.

ABOVE: Drugs of all kinds become available, although illegal in the decade that turns on, tunes in, and drops out.

UDI IN RHODESIA

The minority white government of Southern Rhodesia, led by Ian Smith, makes a unilateral declaration of independence (UDI) from Britain. Britain declares the regime illegal and imposes sanctions. In December 1972, the black independence movements ZANU and ZAPU will launch a concerted campaign against Rhodesia with Soviet and Chinese support. The war will end with ZANU, under Robert Mugabe, gaining power. Rhodesia will become Zimbabwe.

WAR IN THE DESERT

War breaks out in Dhofar and Oman between the Sultan's armed forces, with British assistance. The Communist Dhofar Liberation Front later becomes part of the People's Front for the Liberation of the Occupied Arabian Gulf (PFLOAG). Between 1971 and 1975, the Sultan of Oman's forces casualties are 187 killed and 559 wounded.

CLOSELY OBSERVED TRAINS

Czech writer Bohumil Hrabal becomes famous for this short novel about Milos Hrma, a railroad worker who watches as the Nazis transport troops through Czechoslovakia to the Eastern Front. It will be made into a film directed by Jiri Menzel in 1966.

SALK INSTITUTE LABORATORIES

The handling of concrete masses marks this building in La Jolla, California, as one of American architect Louis Kahn's major achievements. The planning, with mechanical services on their own lower floors to give uninterrupted floor space in the labs, is also innovative.

OLD MAP OF A NEW CONTINENT

A parchment map drawn in 1440, 52 years before Columbus reached America, is found. It shows a large island west of Greenland called "Vinland." This is Newfoundland, the land discovered by Norse explorers Bjarni and Leif Eriksson, who crossed the Western Ocean in the 11th century.

FIRST SPACE WALKS

On March 18, Soviet cosmonaut Aleksei Leonov makes the first "space walk," floating free while tethered to his spaceship *Voskhod II*. He stays outside the spaceship for ten minutes. U.S. astronaut Edward H. White makes a space walk on June 3, which lasts four minutes longer.

EARLY BIRD FLIES

On April 6, *Early Bird* (later called *Intelsat 1*), the first geostationary communications satellite, is launched from the United States. It provides a constant communications link between Europe and North America.

COMPUTERS SHRINK

The first so-called "mini-computer" is introduced in the United States; it has 4k of memory and costs a mere $18,000.

TURN ON, TUNE IN ...

Timothy Leary, former professor of Psychology at Harvard University, publishes *The Psychedelic Reader*. He urges readers to "turn on" to narcotic and psychedelic drugs, "tune in, and drop out." He had been dismissed in 1963 for experimenting with the hallucinogen LSD.

ABOVE: Julie Andrews stars in the blockbuster *The Sound of Music*.

CHARLES-EDOUARD JEANNERET (LE CORBUSIER) (1887–1965)

Swiss-born French architect and town planner Charles-Edouard Jeanneret, better known as Le Corbusier, has died. He was one of the most influential architects of the modern movement, dedicated to developing architectural forms for the machine age, and deviser of the modular system (which uses standard units in building). His buildings include the Unité d'Habitation at Marseilles (1945–1950) and he worked on the town plan and the Law Court and Secretariat buildings at Chandigarh, India (1951–1956). His writings include *Towards a New Architecture* (1923).

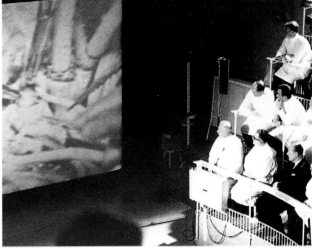

ABOVE: Open heart surgery being performed in Houston, Texas, can be seen live in Geneva, Switzerland, thanks to transmission via the U.S. *Early Bird* communications satellite.

LEFT: During the Cultural Revolution in China, the population suffers intimidation at the hands of the Red Guard under the direction of Chairman Mao.

SURFING THE SLOPES
An engineer in Michigan takes his daughter's sled and adds "footstops" to create a sled you can stand on. He christens it the "Snurfer." Unwittingly, Sherman Poppen has created the snowboard, which now challenges traditional skis on slopes around the world.

HARE KRISHNA
The International Society of Krishna Consciousness is founded in New York City by A.C. Bhaktivedanta, a Sanskrit scholar and chemist who arrived from Calcutta with $50 in rupees and a pair of cymbals to spread Lord Krishna's word. His young followers shave their heads, wear saffron-colored robes, and chant.

BABY RACERS
The lightweight, collapsible McLaren baby buggy appears.

SOFT FOCUS
Soft contact lenses are added to improvements in vision correction recently introduced. They include the omnifocal lens, developed in 1963, which allows close-up and distant vision without disruption.

ASTROTURF
Baseball's Houston Astros become the first team to play on Astroturf. Their ground, the Astrodome in Houston, is enclosed. Clear glass panels in the roof are supposed to allow natural grass to grow. Fielders, however, are blinded by the glare of the sun when trying to catch high balls and so the panels have to be painted, killing the grass. A new artificial surface, named after the building and team, is used instead.

WINSTON LEONARD SPENCER CHURCHILL (1874–1965)

The venerable English statesman and wartime leader Sir Winston Leonard Spencer Churchill has died. Crowds line the streets to witness his funeral procession. He began his parliamentary career in 1900, was Conservative chancellor of the exchequer in 1924–1929, and on the stepping down of Neville Chamberlain, formed the wartime Coalition Government. As British prime minister from 1940–1945, he used his powers of oratory to make morale-boosting broadcasts to the nation. He served again as prime minister during the days of postwar recovery, from 1951 until 1955.

FLOODS AND HAPPENINGS

Indira Gandhi takes the helm of the Indian government and Prime Minister Hendrik Verwoerd of South Africa is assassinated. Civil war breaks out in the Dominican Republic and the Marines are sent in. Priceless Italian art treasures are lost or damaged in floods that devastate Venice and Florence. Russian and American unmanned space probes land on the Moon at last. Back on earth, an H-bomb is lost at sea (but recovered), fiber optics are introduced, and the art world unveils the Happening.

1 9 6 6

Jan	11	Indira Gandhi becomes India's prime minister following the death of Lal Bahandra Shastri
Feb	1	Actor Buster Keaton dies at the age of 70 and gossip columnist Hedda Hopper dies at 75
	3	Soviet space probe makes a soft landing on the Moon
	14	Australia adopts decimal currency
Mar	29	Leonid Brezhnev takes his position as First Secretary of the Soviet Communist Party
	31	The Labour Party wins a decisive victory in the U.K. general election with a majority of 96
Apr	24	Civil war breaks out in the Dominican Republic

May	26	British Guiana becomes independent as Guyana
June	3	U.S. space probe makes a soft landing on the Moon
	13	The Supreme Court rules in Miranda v Arizona that the accused must be informed of their rights prior to interrogation
July	23	Actor Montgomery Clift dies at age 45
Sep	6	South African prime minister Hendrik Verwoerd is assassinated in parliament
	13	B. J. Vorster becomes South African prime minister
Dec	15	Cartoon king Walt Disney dies at age 65

GANDHI BECOMES PRIME MINISTER

Indira Gandhi, daughter of Nehru, becomes prime minister of India after the unexpected death of Lal Shastri.

INDEPENDENCE IN AFRICA AND THE CARIBBEAN

Guyana gains its independence from Britain, followed by Botswana, Lesotho, and Barbados. Seven other Caribbean islands, plus Belize, will gain their independence from Britain by 1983.

DOMINICAN REPUBLIC CIVIL WAR

Some 20,000 U.S. forces intervene in the civil war to restore peace following a coup that overthrows President Juan Bosch. In the fighting, more than 2,000 Dominicans are killed. By October 1966, new elections will bring stability and U.S. forces withdraw.

VERWOERD ASSASSINATED

South African prime minister Hendrik Verwoerd, a firm supporter of apartheid, is stabbed to death in Cape Town's parliament by a lone assassin. He is succeeded by Balthasar Johannes Vorster.

MOON PICTURES

Within months of each other, Soviet and American space probes make soft landings on the Moon. Both take photographs of the surface, enabling both sides of the Moon to be mapped for the first time.

YAMANASHI CENTER

Japanese architect Kenzo Tange designs this center in Kofu, Japan, for press and broadcasting. It uses an innovative structure in which office spaces are supported by 16 massive concrete tubes, each some 16 feet wide. The structure gives the building a unique appearance and character.

DOCKING IN SPACE

Aboard the *Gemini 8*, U.S. astronauts Neil Armstrong and David Scott dock with the final stage of their rocket, but a technical error means the docking is not entirely successful. The ability to dock in orbit is essential to any attempt to land on the Moon.

THE BASSARIDS

German composer Hans Werner Henze reworks Euripides' ancient drama *The Bacchae* in what he feels to be his finest opera. Rational, disciplined King Pentheus (possibly an emblem of Nazism) is overcome by irrational Dionysus.

COOKING ON CHINA

The ceramic stove, a flat surface consisting of hot plates and cool surrounding areas, is introduced by Corning Glass Works. It is patterned to indicate the position of the hot plates and heated by electric elements beneath.

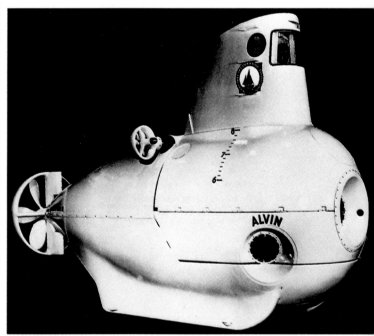

ABOVE: A cable-controlled underwater research vehicle (top) and *Alvin* the midget sub find and recover an H-bomb lost at sea.

AGAINST INTERPRETATION

In this, the first of several influential books of essays, American writer Susan Sontag ranges over many subjects including art, film, music, and politics. This work confirms her stature as one of America's new intellectuals.

PHONING BY GLASS

British scientists Charles Kao and George Hockham invent telephone cables made of glass optical fibers. Fiber optics make it possible for many more calls to be transmitted along a single cable.

FLOODS IN ITALY

Venice is flooded when high waters in the Adriatic cause the Venetian Lagoon to rise above its normal level. Storms in northern Italy cause the Arno River to burst its banks, flooding the city of Florence. Ancient buildings, frescoes, paintings, sculptures, and books are damaged.

IT'S ALL HAPPENING
The "Happening," a form of performance art, is introduced by American painter Robert Rauschenberg at the New York Armory Show. It is the first of many.

LOST H-BOMB FOUND
A hydrogen bomb inadvertently falls off a U.S. bomber in February. Fortunately for all concerned, it is found intact on the Atlantic seabed two months later and is carefully recovered.

DEATHS IN THE PERFORMING ARTS
American comic genius of the silent screen Buster Keaton (b. 1886) dies, as does poet André Breton (also born in 1886), founder of the surrealist movement.

ON AGGRESSION
Austrian biologist Konrad Lorenz publishes this controversial book. His pioneering studies in ethology (animals in their environment) lead him to conclude that some aspects of animal and human aggression are innate. In *King Solomon's Ring*, published in 1963, he had argued controversially that Darwinian natural selection determines behavioral characteristics of animals.

WALTER ELIAS (WALT) DISNEY
(1901–1966)

The death of Walt Disney is announced. The American cartoon filmmaker has given us such characters as Donald Duck and Mickey Mouse and the first color animated film, *Snow White and the Seven Dwarfs* (1937). This was followed by *Fantasia (1940) Pinocchio* (1940) *Bambi* (1943) *Lady and the Tramp* (1956), and many more. He opened his theme park, Disneyland, in Anaheim, California in 1955.

LEFT: Walt Disney dies at 65. In addition to his well-known cartoon characters, he also produced colored nature and adventure films.

BELOW: A model of Boeing's version of a supersonic aircraft. It does not take off from the drawing board.

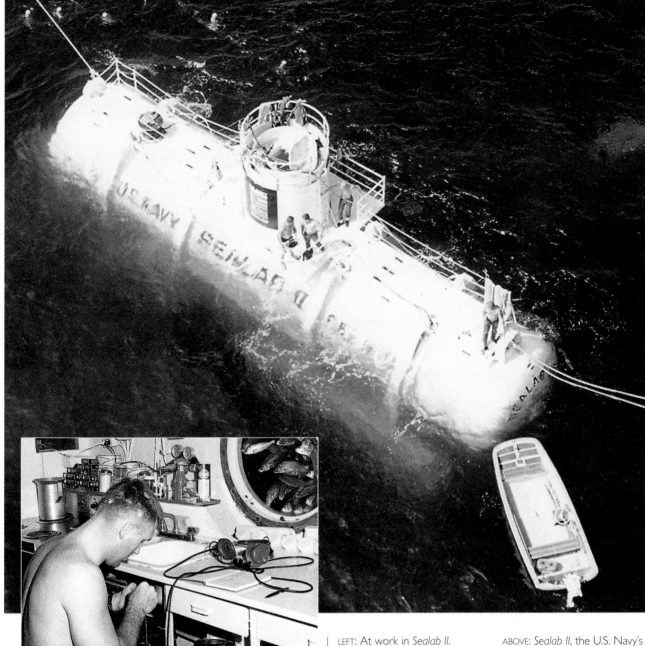

LEFT: At work in *Sealab II*. The fish find it fascinating.

ABOVE: *Sealab II*, the U.S. Navy's underwater research station.

CLEAN AND GREEN

Biodegradable liquid detergents are introduced. They are considered to be better for the environment.

GERMANY THOUGHT IT WAS OVER

England uses home field advantage to win the soccer World Cup for the first time. A thrilling final goes into overtime before England beats the Germans 4–2, thanks to a hat trick from Geoff Hurst.

FOOD CRISIS

A world food crisis has resulted from prolonged drought in Asia and the Sahel, harvest failures in the Soviet Union, and rapid world population growth. High-yielding dwarf indica rice is introduced into Asian countries where there is widespread starvation.

BELOW: Cuban refugees are picked up off the coast of Florida.

THE SUMMER OF LOVE

The Monterey Pop Festival inaugurates the summer of love. In the United States and Europe, the air is alive with the scent of flowers and the tinkle of bells. Civil war tears Nigeria apart and Israel fights and wins the Six-Day War. America's Vietnam involvement attracts escalating protest in the United States and elsewhere. There are many marches and demonstrations. The military takes over Greece and both competitors in the space race suffer their first tragedies. Handsome, charismatic revolutionary Che Guevara is killed and his image becomes a poster icon for the age.

1967

Jan	27	Three U.S. astronauts die when their spacecraft catches fire during tests
Apr	19	Former German chancellor Konrad Adenauer dies at age 91
	21	Junta of colonels takes over Greece following a military coup
	24	Soviet cosmonaut Vladimir Komorov dies when his spacecraft's parachute fails on landing
May	26	Civil war starts in Nigeria after Biafra breaks away
	28	U.K. yachtsman Francis Chichester completes the first solo around the world voyage
	30	President Nasser of Egypt warns Israel of war if it attacks Syria or Egypt
June	5	The Six-Day War begins. Israel defeats coalition of five Arab states
June	29	Actress Jayne Mansfield was decapitated in a car accident near New Orleans
July	1	EEC, European Coal and Steel Community, and Euratom merge to form the European Community (EC)
	22	Poet and author Carl Sandburg dies at the age of 89
	24	President Charles de Gaulle of France angers Canada during visit by supporting independence for Quebec
Oct	3	Folksinger Woody Guthrie dies at the age of 55
	9	Revolutionary guerrilla leader Che Guevara is killed in Bolivia
Dec	3	First human heart transplant performed in South Africa; patient lives only 18 days

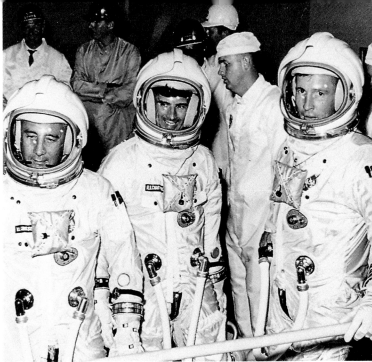

SPACE TEST BAN

The treaty banning nuclear weapons from outer space is signed by the United States, the Soviet Union, and 60 other nations.

GREECE UNDER MILITARY RULE

A junta of right-wing colonels, led by Colonel Georges Papadopoulos, takes military power in Greece and overthrows the civilian government.

CIVIL WAR IN NIGERIA

Following a military coup and tribal discord, the predominantly Ibo eastern region of Nigeria declares unilateral independence as the Republic of Biafra, under Lieutenant Colonel Odemegu Ojukwu. The Nigerian Federal government launches ground and air attacks. Many refugees flee the fighting and starvation causes many deaths, until the rebellion collapses in January 1970 with the fall of Owerri and the victory of the Nigerian Army. Biafra loses 200,000 dead from starvation and fighting and Nigerian casualties are estimated at 10,000 dead.

THE SIX-DAY WAR

In a preemptive strike against its Arab neighbors, which had been threatening its borders, Israel invades Egypt, Jordan, and Syria in a rapid six-day war, establishing new borders on the Suez Canal and in Jordan, gaining the strategic Golan Heights, and re-uniting the city of Jerusalem. The Israelis lose 679 killed: the Arabs lose 3,000 dead, 6,000 wounded, and 12,000 prisoners. Refugees from the West Bank territories of Jordan form the basis for the Palestine Liberation Organization (PLO) which becomes the umbrella organization for attacks on Israel.

EUROPE UNITES

The European Community (EC) is formed out of the European Economic Community (EEC), the European Coal and Steel Community (ECSC), and Euratom. In December, France vetoes the second application for membership by Britain.

ANTI-VIETNAM RALLY

In Washington, antiwar protesters, novelist Norman Mailer and poet Robert Lowell among them, surround the Pentagon. Soldiers and police drive them back with nightsticks and rifle butts and 250 people are arrested. Anti-Vietnam marches and rallies will proliferate all over America and Europe until the war ends.

QUEBEC LIBRE

French president Charles de Gaulle stirs up Quebec nationalism on a visit to Canada by supporting a free Quebec.

CHE KILLED

Argentinian-born Marxist and co-architect of the Cuban Revolution, Ernesto "Che" Guevara, is killed in Bolivia, trying to start a revolution against the government. He becomes an icon of student revolutionaries everywhere.

LOST LEADER

Australian prime minister Harold Holt is missing and presumed drowned, after swimming off the coast at Portsea in Victoria.

ONE HUNDRED YEARS OF SOLITUDE

Colombian writer Gabriel García Márquez's novel depicts a decaying village from the viewpoint of seven generations of one family. In the novel, the magical and fantastic can happen alongside real, everyday events, and every detail glows with significance. This makes the book the key text in the style known as "magic realism".

BLUEBIRD OF TRAGEDY

British racer Donald Campbell is killed on Coniston Water in the Lake District in an attempt to break the world water speed record in his jet-powered vehicle.

HOMOSEXUALITY LEGALIZED
Homosexuality is decriminalized in Britain by the Sexual Offenses Act, which legalizes sex between consenting adult men aged 21 or over.

DEATH OF A PHYSICIST
J. Robert Oppenheimer (b. 1904) dies. A nuclear physicist, he was part of the team that developed and built the atom bomb, but resigned in 1945 protesting against its use on Hiroshima and Nagasaki.

THE MEDIUM IS THE MESSAGE
In the sociological-philosophical tract, *The Medium is the Message*, Canadians Marshall McLuhan and Quentin Fiore analyze popular culture, media, and the impact of printing on civilization. The work has a strong influence on thinking about everything from advertising to literature. The book's title introduces a new buzzword into the language. McLuhan is also responsible for the concept of the "global village," referring to the proliferation of communication methods.

ROSENCRANTZ AND GUILDENSTERN ARE DEAD
Czech-born playwright Tom Stoppard's second play brings him fame and critical attention. Centered on the off-stage lives of two minor characters in Shakespeare's *Hamlet*, it shows the writer's talent for taking an idea and running with it, as well as his resourcefulness with language.

ABOVE: Psychedelic rockers Jim Morrison and The Doors release their seminal album, *Light my Fire*.

SPACE TRAGEDIES
Three U.S. astronauts — Roger B. Chaffee, Virgil I. Grissom, and Edward H. White — are killed during a ground test of an Apollo spacecraft, which catches fire. The Soviet spacecraft *Soyuz I* crashes to the ground when its parachute tangles on reentry. Cosmonaut Vladimir M. Komarov is killed.

ANOTHER NEW ELEMENT
The artificial radioactive element 105 is produced by Russian scientists and they propose to name it nielsbohrium. American scientists also produce it and call it hahnium. Neither name has been accepted.

DEATHS IN THE ARTS
British actress Vivien Leigh (b. 1913), American jazzman John Coltrane (b. 1926), writer and critic Dorothy Parker (b. 1893), actress Jayne Mansfield (b. 1932), actor Spencer Tracy (b. 1900), and French writer André Maurois (b. 1885) all die during this year.

THE FASHION FOR JOGGING
The book *Jogging*, by University of Oregon athletics coach Bill Bowerman, helps create the jogging and running craze. Bowerman had observed jogging programs for health and fitness in New Zealand and uses the ideas in his book.

PULSARS DISCOVERED

British astronomer Jocelyn Bell Burnell discovers pulsating stars (later called pulsars), using a multidish radio telescope she helped to build at Cambridge University, England.

NOVEMBER STEPS

Japanese composer Toru Takemitsu's *November Steps* is performed for the first time. Written for a Western orchestra and two Japanese instruments, the *biwa* and *shakuhachi*, it brings together Japanese and Western classical musical traditions and is regarded as his most important work.

EXPO 67

Expo 67 opens in Montreal to celebrate Canada's centenary on December 31, 1966. The Canadian pavilion is an inverted pyramid named Katimavik, the Inuit word for "meeting place." America displays contemporary art in a geodesic dome. Israeli-born Canadian architect Moshe Safde celebrates "a sense of house" in an imaginative apartment house with private outdoor space. This apartment house is made up of hundreds of prefabricated containers, held together by steel cables. The design allows other containers to be added at later dates. The house shows the scope of prefabrication.

ADEN INDEPENDENT

Britain grants independence to Aden, in Yemen, its last Middle East colony, after many years of local revolt.

FIRST HUMAN HEART TRANSPLANT

South African surgeon Christiaan Barnard performs the first human heart transplant at Grote Schuur hospital. However, the patient, Louis Washkansky, dies from pneumonia 18 days later.

THE SUMMER OF LOVE

The Monterey Pop Festival in San Francisco marks the beginning of the hippie "Summer of Love." It spreads to London, where pop festivals are held in Hyde Park, and to Amsterdam, Europe's capital of alternative culture.

ABORTION REFORM

Abortion is legalized in Britain under medical supervision and subject to specified criteria. Sweden, Denmark, and Iceland legalized abortion on several grounds before World War II, but Britain is the first Western European country to do so. Colorado also legalizes abortion this year.

THE NAKED APE

Published by British zoologist Desmond Morris, this book interprets aspects of human behavior, such as hunting instincts, pair-bonding, mutual grooming, and territoriality, with the behavior of animals, especially that of apes.

KONRAD ADENAUER
(1876–1967)

German elder statesman Konrad Adenauer has died. Adenauer, whose political career began as Lord Mayor of Cologne in 1917, was dismissed from office and imprisoned by the Nazis. He was reinstated by the Allies in 1945, when he founded the Christian Democratic Union. He was chancellor of the Federal Republic of Germany from 1949 to 1963.

SUPER BOWL

The Green Bay Packers of the National Football League rout the Kansas City Chiefs of the American Football League 35–10 in Super Bowl I. The Super Bowl matches the champions of the two leagues after the merger of the bodies in 1966. The concept is not an immediate success and the game is not a sellout.

COGNITIVE PSYCHOLOGY

In the theory put forward in this book, American psychologist Ulric Neisser focuses on analyzing mental processes such as memory and perception, through which we acquire knowledge, rather than observing human behavior. Neisser believes we use our experience to build models (called "schemas"), which we use to analyze impressions and anticipate what might happen.

ELEMENTS OF SEMIOLOGY

French philosopher Roland Barthes (1915–1980) develops the idea that any product of culture, from language and literature to dress and children's toys, is a system of signs which together provide a means of interpreting and understanding the culture.

NUCLEAR FOOD

The U.S. Department of Agriculture begins a test project of irradiating wheat and other foods to kill insects.

SAILING AROUND THE WORLD

British yachtsman Francis Chichester completes a solo circumnavigation of the world in *Gypsy Moth IV*.

RENE FRANÇOIS GHISLAIN MAGRITTE
(1898–1967)

Belgian surrealist painter René Magritte has died. In 1924, he became a member of the newly founded Belgian Surrealist Group. He continued to produce bizarre but meticulously painted works depicting incongruously juxtaposed objects, such as the neat bowler-hatted men dripping from the sky in *Golconda* (1953).

VIETNAM WAR

With the exception of the Civil War, the Vietnam War is the most divisive war ever fought by the United States. Under four presidents, the United States is drawn into the war between North and South Vietnam and then struggles to withdraw with dignity. It begins on July 8, 1959, when unprecedented numbers of "military observers" are sent into South Vietnam by the United States and escalates into full-scale war in 1964. During the war, the South Vietnamese suffer 150,000 killed and 400,000 wounded while the North Vietnamese and Vietcong suffer 100,000 killed and 300,000 wounded. Between January 1, 1961 and January 27, 1972, the United States suffers 45,941 killed and 300,635 wounded. The war lasts until April 30, 1975 and is very unpopular with the American people.

LEFT: American troops from a reconnaissance patrol discover part of the network of tunnels the Vietcong use as a strategic base.

❖KEY DATES❖
IN THE VIETNAM WAR

U.S. ATTACKS Aug 5, 1964
Aircraft from the USS *Constellation* and *Ticonderoga* attack North Vietnamese torpedo boat bases.

"ROLLING THUNDER" Mar 2, 1965
This operation is the first of major U.S.A.F. and U.S. Navy air attacks on North Vietnam. On March 8, 1965, the first U.S. Marines arrive in South Vietnam.

KHE SANH Jan 22–Apr 14, 1968
Some 6,000 U.S. Marines and South Vietnamese troops with 46 guns held a mountain base against 15,000 men in three North Vietnamese divisions.

TET OFFENSIVE Jan 30–31, 1968
The attempt by the Vietcong and North Vietnamese to score a major victory over the United States and South Vietnam cost them 46,000 dead and 9,000 wounded. South Vietnam suffers 2,788 killed and 8,886 wounded and the U.S. forces 1,536 killed and 7,775 wounded. It is a military defeat for the North, but a political victory.

LAM SON 719 Feb 8–Apr 9, 1971
The South Vietnamese unsuccessfully thrust into Laos to disrupt supplies down the Ho Chi Minh Trail. U.S. forces suffer 176 killed and 1,942 wounded. South Vietnam 1,483 killed, 5,420 wounded, and 691 missing. North Vietnam's casualties are 13,636 killed and 69 captured.

ABOVE: Fighting takes place on the streets and is equally as dangerous as jungle warfare.

ABOVE: The chop of helicopter rotor blades is the defining soundtrack to the war in Vietnam.

ABOVE: South Vietnamese civilians run from the scene of a skirmish in which three Vietcong soldiers have been killed.

ABOVE: U.S. Marines move cautiously through flooded rice paddies on a search and clear mission, Operation Deckhouse.

FIGHTING IN THE STREETS

A year of violence and confrontation as the Prague Spring in Czechoslovakia is stifled by Soviet tanks. Martin Luther King, Jr. and Senator Robert Kennedy are gunned down and student revolutionaries take to the streets of Paris. In Vietnam, the Vietcong throw all their energy and fire power into the Tet Offensive. The American retaliation causes protest at home. In Northern Ireland, civil disobedience initiates what will be decades of troubles. The Olympic Games are held in Mexico and are memorable for the Black Power salute given defiantly by black athletes.

1968

Jan	5	Reformer Alexander Dubcek becomes head of the Czech Communist party
	30	Viet Cong launch the Tet Offensive on South Vietnam breaking the New Year truce
	30	North Korea seizes the *Pueblo*, a Navy intelligence ship on patrol off the coast of North Korea
Feb	6	The 10th Winter Olympics open in Grenoble, France
Apr	4	U.S. black leader Martin Luther King, Jr., is assassinated at The Lorraine Hotel in Memphis, Tennessee at the age of 39
May	2	Demonstrating students in Paris begin series of clashes with police
June	5	U.S. senator Robert F. Kennedy is shot in Los Angeles; he dies the next day
July	6	Sixty-one nations sign a treaty on the nonproliferation of nuclear weapons
Aug	20	Soviet and allied troops invade Czechoslovakia to stop Dubcek's reforms
Oct	5	Civil rights demonstrators in Londonderry, Northern Ireland, clash with police for 2 days
	12	The 19th Olympic Games open in Mexico City
Nov	5	Republican Richard M. Nixon is elected U.S. President

LEFT: Civil rights leader Martin Luther King, Jr. is assassinated this year, provoking an outbreak of angry scenes and rioting (above).

LEFT: Civil rights leader Martin Luther King, Jr. is assassinated this year, provoking an outbreak of angry scenes and rioting (above).

SPRINGTIME IN PRAGUE
Alexander Dubcek becomes first secretary of the Czechoslovak Communist Party in January and begins the reforms known as the Prague Spring. Seven months later, Soviet and allied troops invade the country to stop reform. The reforms are abandoned, but Dubcek retains power until he is deposed in April 1969. He later becomes ambassador to Turkey.

DEATH OF A DREAM
Civil rights leader Martin Luther King, Jr. is shot in a motel by an unknown gunman in Memphis, Tennessee. His death leads to major race riots across America.

ANOTHER KENNEDY SHOT
Leading Democratic politician, and brother of the former president, Robert Kennedy is shot and killed after winning the primary election in California. His death leads to widespread disillusionment in the United States and results in the victory of the Republican candidate Richard Nixon in November's presidential election.

ABOVE: "Earthrise," as seen and photographed by the U.S. astronauts who orbit the Moon in *Apollo 8* in December of this year.

ABOVE: Mrs. Coretta Scott King is speaking in front of the Lincoln Memorial in Washington, D.C., after the death of her husband.

TET OFFENSIVE

The Vietcong use the lull of the Tet (New Year) holiday to launch a multitargeted offensive on Saigon and other strategic ares of the country. They occupy the U.S. embassy in Saigon and capture Hue. The United States and South Vietnam fight back and retake Hue in February, but the retaliation, which is televised and involves civilian executions, has a disastrous effect on U.S. morale at home.

SINFONIA

Italian composer Luciano Berio writes *Sinfonia* for the virtuoso vocal group, the Swingle Singers. Full of quotations, both musical and verbal, and references to recent events (the student unrest in Paris), the work finally comes to rest in a meditation on the life and death of Martin Luther King, Jr.

NONPROLIFERATION PACT

In London, 61 nations, including Britain, the U.S.S.R., and the United States, sign the Nuclear Nonproliferation Treaty, which prohibits the spread of nuclear weapons.

BELOW: Plastic research balloons are sent up into the stratosphere to collect data for the National Center for Atmospheric Research.

LES EVENEMENTS

French students protesting against the Vietnam War and other grievances occupy their universities and take their protests to the streets. Barricades are erected in Paris and the government almost falls. The protests are copied by students throughout Europe and the United States. Violent demonstrations take place against the autocratic structure of universities across Europe, from Britain to West Germany. The French universities close after demonstrations at the University of Nanterre spread to the Sorbonne in Paris. In the Netherlands, the Maris Report, calling for extensive centralization of university resources, leads to demonstrations in Utrecht, Delft, Wageningen, Groningen, and, later, Amsterdam.

TROUBLE IN IRELAND

Disturbances break out as civil rights demonstrators protesting against anti-Catholic discrimination by the Protestant majority government clash with police. In the next few months, civil rights demonstrators increase their agitation across the province. The minority Catholic population has not enjoyed full civil rights since the 1922 partition of Ireland. Rioting in Londonderry cannot be contained by the Royal Ulster Constabulary (RUC) and the British government sends in troops to regain control.

MILE-LONG DRAWING

Two parallel lines on the desert floor make up Walter de Maria's Mile-Long Drawing. It is an early work of conceptual art and also an early example of making art on and out of the land.

ASTRONAUTS ORBIT THE MOON

In December, the U.S. *Apollo 8* becomes the first manned capsule to orbit the Moon. The spacecraft, carrying astronauts Frank Borman, James A. Lovell, and William A. Anders, reaches the moon on Christmas eve and makes ten orbits in twenty hours before returning safely to the Pacific Ocean.

ABOVE: Robert F. Kennedy is assassinated this year by a Jordanian student, Sirhan Bissara Sirhan.

PULSARS IDENTIFIED
U.S. astronomer Thomas Gold discovers that pulsars, first observed in 1967, are actually neutron stars. These are formed of closely packed neutrons and are the densest known stars.

REGULAR HOVERCRAFT SERVICE
The first regular hovercraft service across the English Channel, from Dover to Boulogne, begins. The N4 hovercraft carries 254 passengers and 30 cars.

OIL IN ALASKA
U.S. petroleum companies discover a huge oil field at Prudhoe Bay, on the Arctic Sea coast of north Alaska.

CLEANER WALLS
Washable wallpaper is manufactured by Du Pont in the United States. It is made from polythene and resists tearing. A flexible fabric version is used to make disposable underwear and uniforms.

WIMBLEDON OPENS TO PROFESSIONALS
Rod Laver takes the inaugural Open Wimbledon. After a long struggle in the face of rising professionalism, the tournament allows professional tennis players to participate for the first time.

BLACK POWER OLYMPICS
The 19th Olympics in Mexico are filled with stunning performances and powerful protest. The altitude of Mexico City gives an advantage in sprint events and 34 world records and 38 Olympic records are set. American Bob Beamon smashes the long jump record by 55cm and his compatriot Jim Hines wins the 100m in 9.95 seconds. Fellow sprinters Tommie Smith and John Carlos create the image of the games, however, when they raise black-fisted gloves on the medal podium in a salute to black power. The U.S. team sends the 200m medal winners home, but the world sees their protest. Dick Fosbury of America transforms the high jump with the technique that becomes known as the "Fosbury Flop."

ABOVE: Day-to-day images such as this wounded American soldier appear daily on television and help to bring an end to the war.

WINTER OLYMPICS IN FRANCE
Events at the 10th Winter Olympics center on Grenoble in France, but events are spread over the surrounding area and seven "villages" host competitors. Drug tests after each event make an appearance. French skier Jean-Claude Killy makes home crowds happy with three skiing golds.

SUPERTANKERS
The first supertankers, giant oceangoing ships for carrying petroleum, come into general use.

MARCEL DUCHAMP
(1887–1968)

French-born American artist Marcel Duchamp, pioneer of dadaism and surrealism, has died. He moved to the United States in 1915 and shocked the art world with "ready-made" works such as his urinal, entitled *Fountain*, of 1917. His work includes *The Large Glass: The Bride Stripped Bare by Her Bachelors Even*, a construction of lead, wire, and tinfoil on a large piece of sheet glass, which he abandoned as uncompleted in 1923 after eight years of work. After this, he concentrated on playing chess.

MOON LANDING AND FLOWER POWER

The year is dominated by the successful U.S. Moon landing and the world watches in awe as astronaut Neil Armstrong takes "one giant leap for mankind." President Nixon initiates the long withdrawal of U.S. troops from Vietnam. In South America, Honduras and El Salvador have a short, fierce war about soccer. Biafra starves as Nigeria blocks aid flights. The open-air rock festival at Woodstock, three days of music, mud, and love, stamps its image on the hearts and minds of a generation.

OPPOSITE: U.S. astronaut Neil Armstrong fulfills President Kennedy's 1961 promise to put an American on the Moon.

1969

Feb	3	Yasser Arafat is appointed head of the Palestine Liberation Organization
	3	Boris Karloff, best known for his role as "Frankenstein," dies at age 81
	9	The American Boeing 747, the world's largest airliner, makes its first flight
Mar	2	Anglo-French Concorde, the first supersonic airliner, makes its trial flight
Apr	23	Sirhan Sirhan is convicted of killing Senator Robert Kennedy
	28	President Charles de Gaulle of France resigns
May	14	President Richard Nixon proposes withdrawal of U.S., Allied, and North Vietnamese troops from South Vietnam

July	1	In Britain, Prince Charles is invested as Prince of Wales
	13	Dispute over football match leads to war between Honduras and El Salvador
	18	Mary Jo Kopechne drowns in an auto accident in a vehicle driven by Senator Edward Kennedy, who left the scene of the accident
	20	U.S. astronaut Neil Armstrong becomes the first man to set foot on the Moon
Aug	19	British troops take over security duty in Northern Ireland
Sep	1	In Libya, Colonel Gaddaffi overthrows King Idris and becomes head of state
	3	President Ho Chi Minh of North Vietnam dies at age 79

ABOVE: President Nixon greets the press in the Socialist Republic of Romania. He is the first U.S. president to visit the country.

TROOPS IN NORTHERN IRELAND
British troops patrol the streets to protect Catholics from attack by Protestant gangs. The troops are sent in as a temporary measure to keep the two communities apart, but are forced to remain longer as the security situation deteriorates.

LIBYAN COUP
King Idris of Libya is toppled in a coup and replaced as head of state by Colonel Muammar Gaddafi, a follower of the political theories of Mao Zedong.

OSTPOLITIK IN GERMANY
The Social Democrats win the general election and Willy Brandt, former mayor of West Berlin, becomes chancellor, the first Social Democrat to lead West Germany. He begins a policy of *Ostpolitik*, or reconciliation with the Eastern bloc.

ISRAEL'S NEW LEADER
Seventy year old Golda Meir becomes the first woman prime minister of Israel.

MANSON FAMILY MURDERS
American actress Sharon Tate (wife of film director Roman Polanski) is found brutally murdered, along with four friends, at her Beverly Hills home. Another couple, Leno Lo Bianca and his wife, are also found dead in the same fashionable district. Eventually Charles Manson, a charismatic ex-convict, and four members of his desert-dwelling hippie family are arrested, tried, and found guilty of the crimes.

SLAUGHTERHOUSE FIVE
Set partly during the bombing of Dresden, American writer Kurt Vonnegut's cult novel cuts through genres. Part science fiction, part anti-war tract, part autobiography, its slangy, surreal approach makes it popular. It remains the best known of Vonnegut's many books.

PALACH'S PROTEST
Jan Palach, Czech philosophy student, sets fire to himself and dies in protest against the Soviet occupation of his country.

THE GENERAL STEPS DOWN
General de Gaulle resigns as president of France after losing a constitutional referendum. The Gaullist Georges Pompidou wins the presidential election in June.

EIGHT SONGS FOR A MAD KING
A key work of "music theater" (not quite opera, not quite concert music), the eight songs by British composer Peter Maxwell Davies are sung by the mad George III, or at least a character who thinks he is the mad George III. The range of musical references (Handel on the honky tonk piano) and the violence of the emotions (and extremes of vocal technique needed to express them) makes the work notorious.

FLOWER POWER
The free music festival on a muddy farm in Woodstock, New York, brings 400,000 people together for a three day celebration of peace, love, and understanding. Major music stars include Jimi Hendrix, The Who, The Band, and Janis Joplin.

TRAGEDY IN BIAFRA
Following the Nigerian ban on aid planes, thousands of people in the breakaway province of Biafra are condemned to die of starvation. Television brings horrific pictures of skeletal children into the homes of the world.

OH, CALCUTTA!
English drama producer and critic Kenneth Tynan's famous musical begins its run in New York City. The satirical work will run for years on Broadway. It contains nude scenes and the title is a pun on the racy French phrase, "O, quel cul tu as" (oh, what a great butt you've got).

MONTY PYTHON'S FLYING CIRCUS

English comic John Cleese and company create a new brand of bizarre humor on television. Acting styles, linguistic wit, and groundbreaking animation all push television humor in new, surreal directions and the Pythons gain popular following in Europe and America. The style will later be even more successful worldwide in a series of films.

ARCHITECTURAL INNOVATORS DIE

Influential German architects Ludwig Mies van der Rohe (b. 1886) and Walter Gropius (b. 1883), founder of the Bauhaus, die during this year.

STONEWALL RIOTS

In New York City, police raid the Stonewall Bar, popular with lesbians and homosexuals. They meet resistance. This marks the beginning of the fight for gay rights.

SUPERSONIC AIRLINERS

In March, the world's first supersonic airliner, the Anglo-French *Concorde 001*, makes its first flight in France. Not to be outdone, Russia's supersonic airliner, the *TU-144* (called "Concordski" by the English-speaking press) makes its first flight two months later.

ANTIBIOTIC BAN

The British Ministry of Agriculture and the American Food and Drug Administration both ban the addition of penicillin and tetracycline antibiotics to livestock feed because of the danger of an increase in drug-resistant bacteria.

METEORITES FOUND IN ANTARCTICA

Japanese geologists find meteorites on the Antarctic ice cap.

OVER THE RAINBOW

Judy Garland (b. 1922), forever remembered as Dorothy in *The Wizard of Oz*, dies in London.

HO CHI MINH
(BORN NGUYEN THAT THANH)
(1890–1969)

Ho Chi Minh, the Vietnamese leader whose name is a household word around the world thanks to the Vietnam War, has died. He was the son of a mandarin. Between 1912 and 1930, he spent much of his life in Britain, the United States, France, and Russia. Founder of the Indo-Chinese Communist party (1930) and the Vietminh Independence League (1941), he led his country against the French (1946–54), and became prime minister of the newly established North Vietnam in 1954. He led the struggle against the U.S.-aided South Vietnam, which developed into war in 1964.

ABOVE: The King is back. Elvis Presley returns to the public stage this year, performing mainly in Las Vegas.

A GIANT STEP FOR MANKIND

U.S. astronaut Neil A. Armstrong becomes the first man to set foot on the Moon; he is followed by Edwin E. "Buzz" Aldrin 18 minutes later. They become the first people to photograph another planet, using modified Hasselblad cameras. The third astronaut, Michael Collins, orbits the Moon in *Apollo 11*, ready to pick the others up and return them to Earth. The whole mission is televised and viewed across the world.

NORTHWEST PASSAGE VOYAGE

The American icebreaking supertanker *Manhattan* makes the first commercial voyage through the Northwest Passage, the seaway around Canada linking the Atlantic and Pacific. The trip takes three months.

SOCCER MAD

El Salvador and Honduras go to war over a soccer game. Honduran citizens attack Salvadorians in Honduras after El Salvador wins a World Cup qualifying game in Mexico. The government of El Salvador retaliates. Fighting lasts a week.

AN ELEPHANT FLIES
The largest commercial jetliner, the Boeing 747, makes its first flight. Popularly known as a jumbo jet, it can carry 362 passengers.

NORTH SEA OIL FOUND
High-grade crude petroleum is found in the northern North Sea between Britain and Norway. The find will mean great prosperity for both countries.

WALKING ON WATER
The British Trans-Arctic Expedition led by Wally Herbert reaches Spitzbergen. Its members become the first people to cross the frozen Arctic Ocean on foot. They have travelled 3,600 miles in 464 days from Point Barrow, Alaska.

OPEN SESAME
Sesame Street begins on American Public Service TV and revolutionizes children's attitudes to learning. Designed by Children's TV Workshop and funded by the Ford Foundation, Carnegie, and the U.S. Office of Education, it uses techniques of commercial television to teach letters and numbers in English and Spanish. Kermit the Frog and other "muppets" make their first appearance.

WORDS OF WARNING
Problems of the Human Environment, commissioned by the United Nations, reports that 1,236 million acres of arable land and two-thirds of the world's original forests have been lost, mainly through poor agricultural management and forest clearances.

OFF THE ROAD
American writer Jack Kerouac (b. 1922), the original "beatnik" and assiduous chronicler of the romance of the road, dies.

POLLUTION SPREADS
Alarm over pollution grows after millions of Rhine fish are killed by leakage from Thiodan 2 insecticide canisters that had been dropped into the river in 1967. In 1968, nerve gas from a U.S. Army site in Utah escapes, killing 6,000 sheep. Next Japan reports cadmium poisoning, Texas reports mercury poisoning, and in Arizona, DDT is found in mothers' milk.

SUPER BOWL SUCCESS
The upstart New York Jets of the junior American Football League beat the Baltimore Colts of the National Football League 16–7 to take the Super Bowl, a win that had been confidently predicted by the Jets' brash quarterback Joe Namath. The Super Bowl becomes America's top sporting occasion.

VOYAGE TO THE MOON

ABOVE: Liftoff for *Apollo 11* on its historic mission to the Moon.

LEFT: The command and service module of *Apollo 11* floats above the Sea of Tranquillity, photographed from the orbiting lunar module.

ABOVE: Safe splashdown for the crew of *Apollo 12*, the second team of U.S. astronauts to walk on the Moon. They are (l to r) Charles Conrad, Jr., Richard F. Gordon, Jr., and Alan L. Bean.

ABOVE: Aboard the USS *Hornet*, President Nixon hails the *Apollo 11* crew on their safe return from the Moon.

MEN ON THE MOON

The 1960s see human beings on the Moon. From the first short space-hops of 1961 to the full-scale multi-teamed expeditions that characterize this year, the whole Moon mission fits neatly into the decade. Using techniques learned on previous missions, *Apollo 11* at last lands the first men on the Moon as the world watches. The mission is followed up by the exploratory team from *Apollo 12* a few months later.

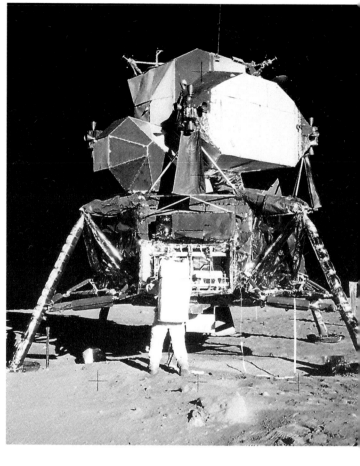

ABOVE LEFT: *Apollo 12* astronaut unpacks the Apollo lunar surface experiments package in the first EVA (extravehicular activity) period of the mission.

ABOVE RIGHT: The fragile-looking *Apollo 12* lunar module. Astronauts Alan Bean and Charles Conrad land on the Moon in this, while Richard Gordon remains with the command and service module in lunar orbit.

LEFT: *Apollo 11* commander Neil Armstrong, photographed by Edwin "Buzz" Aldrin, takes soil samples from the Moon as his first task, in case the expedition is cut short. Armstrong and Aldrin remain on the Moon for just over 21 hours.

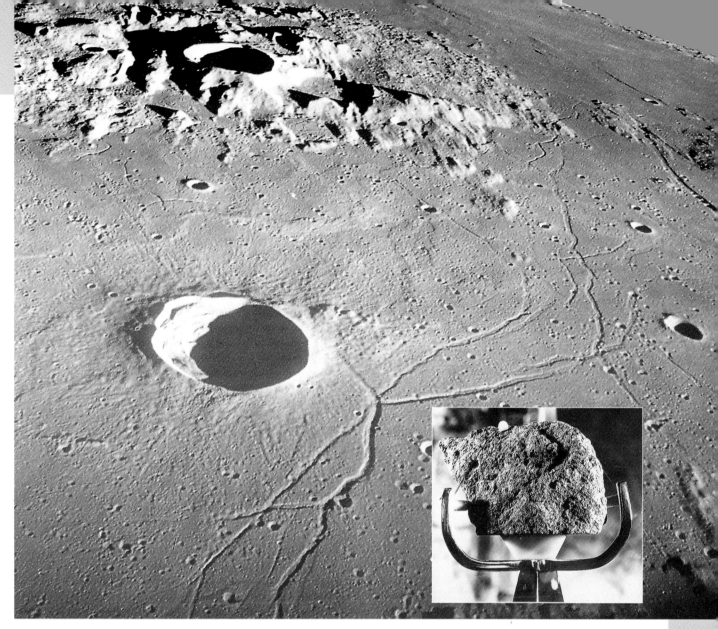

ABOVE: From close up, the Moon's surface appears pock-marked with craters and holes.

INSET: A piece of Moon rock brought back from the *Apollo 12* mission in November. This piece is a form of olivine basalt.

RIGHT: Humanity's first view of its own home, taken from the orbiting lunar module of *Apollo 10*. The blue and green beauty of Earth is a wonderful surprise to many of its inhabitants.

WINNERS AND ACHIEVERS OF THE 1960s

ACADEMY AWARDS
The Academy of Motion Picture Arts and Sciences was founded in 1927 by the movie industry to honor its artists and craftsmen. All categories of motion picture endeavor are honored, but the most significant are listed below.

BEST ACTOR
1960 Burt Lancaster *Elmer Gantry*
1961 Maximilian Schell *Judgment at Nuremberg*
1962 Gregory Peck *To Kill a Mockingbird*
1963 Sidney Poitier *Lilies of the Field*
1964 Rex Harrison *My Fair Lady*
1965 Lee Marvin *Cat Ballou*
1966 Paul Scofield *A Man for All Seasons*
1967 Rod Steiger *In the Heat of the Night*
1968 Cliff Robertson *Charly*
1969 John Wayne *True Grit*

BEST ACTRESS
1960 Elizabeth Taylor *Butterfield 8*
1961 Sophia Loren *Two Women*

1962 Anne Bancroft *The Miracle Worker*
1963 Patricia Neal *Hud*
1964 Julie Andrews *Mary Poppins*
1965 Julie Christie *Darling*
1966 Elizabeth Taylor *Who's Afraid of Virginia Woolf?*
1967 Katharine Hepburn *Guess Who's Coming to Dinner*
1968 Katharine Hepburn *The Lion in Winter*, Barbra Streisand *Funny Girl*
1969 Maggie Smith *The Prime of Miss Jean Brodie*

BEST DIRECTOR
1960 Billy Wilder *The Apartment*
1961 Robert Wise and Jerome Robbins *West Side Story*
1962 David Lean *Lawrence of Arabia*
1963 Tony Richardson *Tom Jones*
1964 George Cukor *My Fair Lady*
1965 Robert Wise *The Sound of Music*
1966 Fred Zinnemann *A Man for All Seasons*
1967 Mike Nichols *The Graduate*
1968 Sir Carol Reed *Oliver!*

1969 John Schlesinger *Midnight Cowboy*

BEST PICTURE
1960 *The Apartment*
1961 *West Side Story*
1962 *Lawrence of Arabia*
1963 *Tom Jones*
1964 *My Fair Lady*
1965 *The Sound of Music*
1966 *A Man for All Seasons*
1967 *In the Heat of the Night*
1968 *Oliver!*
1969 *Midnight Cowboy*

NOBEL PRIZES
The Nobel Prizes are an international award granted in the fields of literature, physics, chemistry, physiology or medicine, and peace. The first prizes were awarded in 1901 and funded by the money left in the will of the Swedish inventor Alfred Nobel (1833–96), who gave the world dynamite.

PRIZES FOR LITERATURE
1960 Saint-John Perse (French) for poetry
1961 Ivo Andric (Yugoslav) for fiction, especially *The Bridge on the Drina.*
1962 John Steinbeck (American) for fiction, especially *The Winter of Our Discontent*
1963 George Seferis (Greek) for lyric poetry
1964 Jean-Paul Sartre (French) for philosophical works (award declined)
1965 Mikhail Sholokhov (Soviet) for fiction
1966 Shmuel Yosef Agnon (Israeli) for stories of Eastern European Jewish life, and Nelly Sachs (German born) for drama and poetry about the Jewish people
1967 Miguel Angel Asturias (Guatemalan) for writings rooted in national individuality and Indian traditions
1968 Yasunari Kawabata (Japanese) for fiction
1969 Samuel Beckett (Irish born) for fiction and drama

PRIZES FOR PEACE
1960 Albert John Luthuli (African) for peaceful campaigning against racial restrictions in South Africa
1961 Dag Hammarskjöld (Swedish) for efforts to bring peace to the Congo (awarded posthumously)
1962 Linus Pauling (American) for efforts to ban nuclear weapons, especially for campaigning against nuclear weapons testing
1963 International Committee of the Red Cross and League of Red Cross Societies for humanitarian work
1964 Martin Luther King, Jr. (American), for leading the black struggle for equality in the United States through non-violent means
1965 United Nations Children's Fund (UNICEF) for its aid to children
1966–1967 *No awards*
1968 René Cassin (French) for promoting human rights
1969 International Labour Organization (ILO) for its efforts to improve working conditions

PRIZES FOR PHYSICS
1960 Donald Glaser (American) for inventing the bubble chamber to study subatomic particles
1961 Robert Hofstadter (American) for studies of nucleons and Rudolf Mossbauer (German) for research on gamma rays
1962 Lev Davidovich Landau (Soviet) for research on liquid helium
1963 Eugene Paul Wigner (American) for contributions to the understanding of atomic nuclei and the elementary particles; and Maria Goeppert Mayer (American) and J Hans Jensen (German) for work on the structure of atomic nuclei
1964 Charles Townes (American) and Nikolai Basov and Alexander Prokhorov (Soviet) for developing masers and lasers

Jon Voight and Dustin Hoffman in *Midnight Cowboy*, 1969.

1965 Sin-itiro Tomonaga (Japanese) and Julian Schwinger and Richard Freyman (American) for basic work in quantum electrodynamics
1966 Alfred Kastler (French) for work on the energy levels of atoms
1967 Hans Albrecht Bethe (American) for contributions to the theory of nuclear reactions, especially discoveries on the energy production in stars
1968 Luis Alvarez (American) for contributions to the knowledge of subatomic particles
1969 Murray Gell-Man (American) for discoveries concerning the classification of nuclear particles and heir interactions

PRIZES FOR CHEMISTRY
1960 Willard F. Libby (American) for developing a method of radiocarbon dating
1961 Melvin Calvin (American) for research on photosynthesis
1962 Sir John Cowdery Kendrew and Max Ferdinand Perutz (British) for studies on globular proteins
1963 Giulio Natta (Italian) for contributions to the understanding of polymers; and Karl Ziegler (German) for the production of organometallic compounds
1964 Dorothy Hodgkin (British) for X-ray studies of compounds such as vitamin B-12 and penicillin
1965 Robert Burns Woodward (American) for contributions to organic synthesis
1966 Robert S. Mulliken (American) for developing the molecular-orbital theory of chemical structure
1967 Manfred Eigen (German) and Ronald Norrish and George Porter (British) for developing techniques to measure rapid chemical reactions
1968 Lars Onsager (American) for developing the theory of reciprocal relations of thermodynamic activity
1969 Derek Barton (British) and Odd Hassel (Norwegian) for studies relating chemical reactions with the three-dimensional shape of molecules

PRIZES FOR PHYSIOLOGY OR MEDICINE
1960 Macfarlane Burnet (Australian) and Peter Medawar (British) for research in transplanting organs
1961 Georg von Bekesy (American) for demonstrating how the ear distinguishes between various sounds
1962 James Watson (American) and Francis Crick and Maurice Wilkins (British) for their work on nucleic acid
1963 Sir John Carew Eccles (Australian) for his research on the transmission of nerve impulses, and Alan Lloyd Hodgkin (British) and Andrew Fielding Huxley (British) for their description of the behavior of nerve impulses
1964 Konrad E. Bloch (American) and Feodor Lynen (German) for work on cholesterol and fatty acid metabolism
1965 François Jacob, André Lwoff and Jacques Monod (French) for their discoveries concerning genetic control of enzyme and virus synthesis
1966 Francis Peyton Rous (American) for discovering a cancer-producing virus, and Charles B. Huggins (American) for discovering uses of hormones in treating cancer
1967 Ragnar Granit (Swedish) and H. Keffer Hartline and George Wald (American) for their work on chemical and physiological processes in the eye
1968 Robert W. Holley, H. Gobind Khorana and Marshall W. Nirenberg (American) for explaining how genes determine the function of cells
1969 Max Delbruck, Alfred Hershey and Salvador Luria (American) for work with bacteriophages

U.S. PRESIDENTS
1953–1961 President Dwight David Eisenhower, *Republican*
1953–1961 Vice President Richard M. Nixon
1961–1963 President John Fitzgerald Kennedy, *Democrat*
1961–1963 Vice President Lyndon Baines Johnson
1963–1969 President Lyndon Baines Johnson, *Democrat*
1965–1969 Vice President Hubert H. Humphrey

1969–1974 President Richard Milhous Nixon, *Republican*
1969–1973 Vice President Spiro T. Agnew
1973–1974 Vice President Gerald R. Ford

SITES OF THE OLYMPIC GAMES
1960 SUMMER Rome, Italy
WINTER Squaw Valley, USA
1964 SUMMER Tokyo, Japan
WINTER Innsbruck, Austria
1968 SUMMER Mexico City
WINTER Grenoble, France

WORLD CUP FINAL MATCHES
YEAR	LOCATION
1962	**Santiago**

Brazil defeats Czechoslovakia 3-1

1966	**London**

England defeats West Germany 4-2

INDIANAPOLIS 500
1960 Jim Rathman
1961 A.J. Foyt, Jr.
1962 Rodger Ward
1963 Parnelli Jones
1964 A.J. Foyt, Jr.
1965 Jim Clark
1966 Graham Hill
1967 A.J. Foyt, Jr.
1968 Bobby Unser
1969 Mario Andretti

KENTUCKY DERBY
1960 Venetian Way
1961 Carry Back
1962 Decidedly
1963 Chateaugay
1964 Northern Dancer
1965 Lucky Debonair
1966 Kauai King
1967 Proud Clarion
1968 Forward Pass
1969 Majestic Prince

NBA CHAMPIONS
1960 Boston Celtics defeat St. Louis Hawks
1961 Boston Celtics defeat St. Louis Hawks
1962 Boston Celtics defeat Los Angeles Lakers
1963 Boston Celtics defeat Los Angeles Lakers
1964 Boston Celtics defeat San Francisco Warriors

1965 Boston Celtics defeat Los Angeles Lakers
1966 Boston Celtics defeat Los Angeles Lakers
1967 Philadelphia 76ers defeat San Francisco Warriors
1968 Boston Celtics defeat Los Angeles Lakers
1969 Boston Celtics defeat Los Angeles Lakers

SUPER BOWL CHAMPIONS
1960–1966 *Not yet played*
1967 Green Bay Packers defeat Kansas City Chiefs 35-10
1968 Green Bay Packers defeat Oakland Raiders 33-14
1969 New York Jets defeat Baltimore Colts 16-7

WIMBLEDON CHAMPIONS
1960 MEN Neale Fraser
WOMEN Maria Bueno
1961 MEN Rod Laver
WOMEN Angela Mortimer
1962 MEN Rod Laver
WOMEN Karen Hantze-Susman
1963 MEN Chuck McKinley
WOMEN Margaret Smith
1964 MEN Roy Emerson
WOMEN Maria Bueno
1965 MEN Roy Emerson
WOMEN Margaret Smith
1966 MEN Manuel Santana
WOMEN Billie Jean King
1967 MEN John Newcombe
WOMEN Billie Jean King
1968 MEN Rod Laver
WOMEN Billie Jean King
1969 MEN Rod Laver
WOMEN Ann Haydon Jones

WORLD SERIES CHAMPIONS
1960 Pittsburgh Pirates defeat New York Yankees
1961 New York Yankees defeat Cincinnati Reds
1962 New York Yankees defeat San Francisco Giants
1963 Los Angeles Dodgers defeat New York Yankees
1964 St. Louis Cardinals defeat New York Yankees
1965 Los Angeles Dodgers defeat Minnesota Twins
1966 Baltimore Orioles defeat Los Angeles Dodgers
1967 St. Louis Cardinals defeat Boston Red Sox
1968 Detroit Tigers defeat St. Louis Cardinals
1969 New York Mets defeat Baltimore Orioles